D0720525

BURN

THIS

BOOK

BURN THIS BOOK

NOTES ON LITERATURE AND ENGAGEMENT

EDITED BY

TONI MORRISON

HARPER

NEW YORK • LONDON • TORONTO • SYDNEY

HARPER

"Peril." Copyright © 2009 by Toni Morrison.

"Why Write?" from *Picked-Up Pieces* by John Updike, copyright © 1975 by John Updike. Used by permission of Alfred A. Knopf, a division of Random House, Inc. Reprinted in the UK with permission of Penguin Books Ltd. Reprinted with permission by Viking Deutsch, 1976.

"Writing in the Dark" from *Writing in the Dark: Essays on Literature and Politics* by David Grossman, translated by Jessica Cohen. Translation copyright © 2008 by Jessica Cohen. Reprinted by permission of Farrar, Straus and Giroux, LLC. Reprinted in the UK by permission of Bloomsbury Publishing.

"Out from Under the Cloud of Unknowing." Copyright © 2008 by Francine Prose.

"The Man, the Men at the Station." Copyright © 2009 by Pico Iyer.

"Notes on Literature and Engagement." Copyright © 2009 by Russell Banks.

"Talking to Strangers." Copyright © 2006 by Paul Auster.

"Freedom to Write," from *Other Colors: Essays and a Story* by Orhan Pamuk, translated by Maureen Freely, translation copyright © 2007 by Maureen Freely. Used by permission of Alfred A. Knopf, a division of Random House, Inc. Copyright © 2006 by Orhan Pamuk; reprinted in the UK with permission of The Wylie Agency LLC. Copyright © 2007 by Orhan Pamuk; reprinted by permission of Knopf Canada.

"Notes on Writing and the Nation" from *Step Across This Line* by Salman Rushdie, copyright © 2002 by Salman Rushdie. Used by permission of Random House, Inc. In the UK, published by Jonathan Cape. Used by permission of The Random House Group Ltd.

"The Sudden Sharp Memory." Copyright © 2009 by Ed Park.

"Witness: The Inward Testimony." Copyright © 2009 by Nadine Gordimer.

"Peril" by Toni Morrison was adapted from an acceptance speech for the 2008 PEN/Borders Literary Service Award. "Writing in the Dark" by David Grossman was adapted from a 2007 PEN speech. "Freedom to Write" by Orhan Pamuk was adapted from a 2006 PEN speech.

A hardcover edition of this book was published in 2009 by HarperStudio, an imprint of HarperCollins Publishers.

HarperCollins books may be purchased for educational, business, or sales promotional use. For information please write: Special Markets Department, HarperCollins Publishers, 10 East 53rd Street, New York, NY 10022.

FIRST HARPER PAPERBACK PUBLISHED 2012.

Designed by Renato Stanisic

Library of Congress Cataloging-in-Publication Data has been applied for.

ISBN 978-0-06-177401-0

12 13 14 15 16   OV/RRD   10 9 8 7 6 5 4 3 2 1

CONTENTS

CONTENTS

BURN THIS BOOK

1

Peril

Toni Morrison

Authoritarian regimes, dictators, despots are often, but not always, fools. But none is foolish enough to give perceptive, dissident writers free range to publish their judgments or follow their creative instincts. They know they do so at their own peril. They are not stupid enough to abandon control (overt or insidious) over media. Their methods include surveillance, censorship, arrest, even slaughter of those writers informing and disturbing the public. Writers who are unsettling, calling into question, taking another, deeper look. Writers—journalists, essayists, bloggers, poets, playwrights—can disturb the social oppression that functions like a coma on the population, a coma despots call peace; and they stanch the blood flow of war that hawks and profiteers thrill to.

That is their peril.

Ours is of another sort.

How bleak, unlivable, insufferable existence becomes when we are deprived of artwork. That the life and work of writers facing peril must be protected is urgent, but along with that urgency we should remind ourselves that their absence, the choking off of a writer's work, its cruel amputation, is of equal peril to us. The rescue we extend to them is a generosity to ourselves.

We all know nations that can be identified by the flight of writers from their shores. These are regimes whose fear of unmonitored writing is justified because truth is trouble. It is trouble for the warmonger, the torturer, the corporate thief, the political hack, the corrupt justice system, and for a comatose public. Unpersecuted, unjailed, unharassed writers are trouble for the ignorant bully, the sly racist, and the predators feeding off the world's resources. The alarm, the disquiet, writers raise is instructive because it is open and vulnerable, because if unpoliced it is threatening. Therefore the historical suppression of writers is the earliest harbinger of the steady peeling away of additional rights and liberties that will follow. The history of persecuted writers is as long as the history of literature itself. And the efforts to censor, starve, regulate, and annihilate us are clear signs that something important has taken place. Cultural and political forces can sweep clean all but the "safe," all but state-approved art.

I have been told that there are two human responses to the perception of chaos: naming and violence. When the chaos is simply the unknown, the
naming can be accomplished effortlessly—a new species, star, formula, equation, prognosis. There is also
mapping, charting, or devising proper nouns for un-
named or stripped-of-names geography, landscape, or
population. When chaos resists, either by reforming
itself or by rebelling against imposed order, violence
is understood to be the most frequent response and
the most rational when confronting the unknown,
the catastrophic, the wild, wanton, or incorrigible.
Rational responses may be censure, incarceration in
holding camps, prisons, or death, singly or in war.
There is however a third response to chaos, which
I have not heard about, which is stillness. Such stillness can be passivity and dumbfoundedness; it can
be paralytic fear. But it can also be art. Those writers plying their craft near to or far from the throne
of raw power, of military power, of empire building
and countinghouses, writers who construct meaning
in the face of chaos must be nurtured, protected. And
it is right that such protection be initiated by other
writers. And it is imperative not only to save the besieged writers but to save ourselves. The thought that
leads me to contemplate with dread the erasure of
other voices, of unwritten novels, poems whispered
or swallowed for fear of being overheard by the wrong
people, outlawed languages flourishing underground,
essayists' questions challenging authority never being

posed, unstaged plays, canceled films—that thought is a nightmare. As though a whole universe is being described in invisible ink.

Certain kinds of trauma visited on peoples are so deep, so cruel, that unlike money, unlike vengeance, even unlike justice, or rights, or the goodwill of others, only writers can translate such trauma and turn sorrow into meaning, sharpening the moral imagination.

A writer's life and work are not a gift to mankind; they are its necessity.

2

Why Write?
John Updike

y title offers me an opportunity to set a record of brevity at this Festival of Arts; for an adequate treatment would be made were I to ask, in turn, "Why not?" and sit down.

But instead I hope to explore, for not too many minutes, the question from the inside of a man who, rather mysteriously to himself, has earned a livelihood for close to twenty years by engaging in the rather selfish and gratuitous activity called "writing." I do *not* propose to examine the rather different question of what use is writing to the society that surrounds and, if he is fortunate, supports the writer. The ancients said the purpose of poetry, of writing, was to entertain and to instruct; Aristotle put forward the still fascinating notion that a dramatic action, however terrible and piteous, carries off at the end, in catharsis, the morbid, personal, subjective impurities of our emotions. The enlargement of sympathy, through identification with the lives of fictional others, is frequently presented as an aim of narrative; D. H. Lawrence, with characteristic fervor, wrote, "And here lies the vast importance of the novel, properly handled. It can inform and lead into new places the flow of our sympathetic consciousness, and can lead our sympathy away in recoil from things that are dead." Kafka wrote that a book is an ax to break the frozen sea within us. The frozen sea within himself, he must have meant; though the ax of Kafka's own art (which, but for Max Brod's posthumous disobedience, Kafka would have taken with him into the grave) has served an analogous purpose for others. This note of pain, of saintly suffering, is a modern one, far removed from the serene and harmonious bards and poets of the courts of olden time. Listen to Flaubert, in one of his letters to Louise Colet:

> I love my work with a love that is frenzied and perverted, as an ascetic loves the hair shirt that scratches his belly. Sometimes, when I am empty, when words don't come, when I find I haven't written a single sentence after scribbling whole pages, I collapse on my couch and lie there dazed, bogged in a swamp of despair, hating myself and blaming myself for this demented pride which makes me pant after a chimera. A quarter of

an hour later everything changes; my heart is pounding with joy. Last Wednesday I had to get up and fetch my handkerchief; tears were streaming down my face. I had been moved by my own writing; the emotion I had conceived, the phrase that rendered it, and satisfaction of having found the phrase—all were causing me to experience the most exquisite pleasure.

Well, if such is the writer at work, one wonders why he doesn't find a pleasanter job; and one also wonders why he appears himself to be the chief market for his own product.

Most people sensibly assume that writing is propaganda. Of course, they admit, there is bad propaganda, like the boy-meets-tractor novels of socialist realism, and old-fashioned propaganda, like Christian melodrama and the capitalist success stories of Horatio Alger or Samuel Smiles. But that some message is intended, wrapped in the story like a piece of crystal carefully mailed in cardboard and excelsior, is not doubted. Scarcely a day passes in my native land that I don't receive some letter from a student or teacher asking me *what I meant to say* in such a book, asking me to elaborate more fully on some sentence I deliberately whittled into minimal shape, or inviting me to speak on some topic, usually theological or sexual, on which it is pleasantly assumed I am an expert. The writer as a hero, as Hemingway or Saint-Exupéry or D'Annunzio, a tradition of which Camus was perhaps the last example, has been replaced in America by the writer as educationist. Most writers teach, a great many teach writing; writing is furiously taught at colleges even as the death knell of the book and the written word is monotonously tolled; any writer, it is assumed, can give a lecture, and the purer products of his academic mind, the "writings" themselves, are sifted and, if found to be of sufficient quality, installed in their places on the assembly belt of study, as objects of educational contemplation.

How dare one confess, to the politely but firmly inquiring letter writer who takes for granted that as a remote but functioning element of his education you are duty-bound to provide the information and elucidating essay that will enable him to complete his term paper, or his Ph.D. thesis, or his critical *opus*—how dare one confess that the absence of a swiftly expressible message is, often, *the* message; that reticence is as important a tool to the writer as expression; that the hasty filling out of a questionnaire is not merely irrelevant but *inimical* to the writer's proper activity; that this activity is rather curiously private and finicking, a matter of exorcism and manufacture rather than of toplofty proclamation; that, to be blunt, the social usefulness of writing matters to him primarily in that it somehow creates a few job opportunities—in Australia, a few government grants—a few opportunities to live as a writer.

Not counting journalists and suppliers of scripts to the media, hardly a hundred American men and women earn their living by writing, in a wealthy nation of two hundred million. Does not then, you ask, such a tiny band of privileged spokesmen owe its country, if not the trophy of a Nobel Prize, at least the benign services of a spiritual aristocracy? Is not the writer's role, indeed, to speak for humanity, as conscience and prophet and servant of the billions not able to speak for themselves? The conception is attractive, and there are some authors, mostly Russian, who have aspired to such grandeur without entirely compromising their gifts. But in general, when a writer such as Sartre or Faulkner becomes a great man, a well-intentioned garrulity replaces the specific witness that has been theirs to give.

THE LAST TIME I dared appear on a platform in a foreign land, it was in Kenya, where I had to confess, under some vigorous questioning from a large white man in the audience, that the general betterment of mankind, and even the improvement of social conditions within my own violently imperfect nation, were *not* my basic motivation as a writer. To be sure, *as a citizen* one votes, attends meetings, subscribes to liberal pieties, pays or withholds taxes, and contributes to charities even more generously than—it turns out—one's own President. But as a writer, for me to attempt to extend my artistic scope into all the areas of my human concern, to substitute nobility of purpose for accuracy of execution, would certainly be to forfeit whatever social usefulness I *do* have. It has befallen a Solzhenitsyn to have experienced the Soviet labor camps; it has befallen Miss Gordimer and Mr. Mtshali to suffer the tensions and paradoxes and outrages of a racist police state; social protest, and a hope of reform, is the very fiber of their witness. But a writer's witness, surely, is of value in its circumstantiality. Solzhenitsyn's visible and brave defiance of the Soviet state is magnificent, but a novel like *The First Circle* affords us more than a blind flash of conditioned and—let's face it—chauvinistic indignation; it affords us entry into an unknown world, it offers a complex and only implicitly indignant portrait of how human beings live under a certain sort of political system. When I think of the claustrophobic and seething gray world of *The First Circle*, I am reminded in texture of Henry Miller's infamous Paris novels. Here, too, we have truth, and an undeniable passion to proclaim the truth—a seedy and repellent yet vital truth—though the human conditions Miller describes are far removed from any hope of political cure. And Miller, in his way, was also a martyr: as with Solzhenitsyn, his works could not be published in his native land.

We must write where we stand; wherever we do stand, there is life; and an imitation of the life we know, however narrow, is our only ground. As I sat on that stage in Kenya, a symbolic American in a corner of that immense range of peoples symbolically called the Third World, I felt guilty and bewildered

that I could not hear in my formidable accuser's oro-
tund phrases anything that had to do with my practice of the writer's profession; I was discomfited that
my concerns—to survive, to improve, to make my
microcosms amusing to me and then to others, to
fail, if fail I must, through neither artistic coward-
ice nor laziness, to catch all the typographical errors
in my proofs, to see that my books appear in jackets
both striking and fairly representative of the contents,
to arrange words and spaces and imagined realities
in patterns never exactly achieved before, to be able
to defend any sentence I publish—I was embarrassed
that my concerns were so ignoble, compared to his.
But, once off the stage (where a writer should rarely
be), I tend to be less apologetic, and even to believe
that my well-intentioned questioner, and the silent
faces in the same audience looking to me to atone
for America's sins real and supposed, and the touching schoolchildren begging me by letter to get them
through the seventh grade—that none of these people
have any felt comprehension of my vocation.

WHY WRITE? AS SOON ask, why rivet? Because a
number of personal accidents drifts us toward the occupation of riveter, which preexists, and, most im-
portantly, the riveting gun exists, and we love it.

Think of a pencil. What a quiet, nimble, slender,
and then stubby wonder-worker he is! At his touch,
worlds leap into being; a tiger with no danger, a

steamroller with no weight, a palace at no cost. All children are alive to the spell of pencil and crayons, of making something, as it were, from nothing; a few children never move out from under this spell, and try to become artists. I was once a rapturous child drawing at the dining-room table, under a stained-glass chandelier that sat like a hat on the swollen orb of my excitement. What is exciting that child, so distant from us in time and space? He appears, from the vantage of this lectern unimaginable to him, to be in the grip of two philosophical perceptions.

One, mimesis demands no displacement; the cat I drew did not have to fight for food or love with the real cat that came to the back porch. I was in drawing *adding* to the world rather than rearranging the finite amount of goods within it. We were a family struggling on the poverty edge of the middle class during the Depression; I was keen to avoid my father's noisy plight within the plague of competition; pencil and paper were cheap, unlike most other toys.

And, two, the world called into being on the penciled paper admitted of connections. An early exercise, whose pleasure returns to me whenever I assemble a collection of prose or poetry or whenever, indeed, I work several disparate incidents or impressions into the shape of a single story, was this: I would draw on one sheet of paper an assortment of objects—flowers, animals, stars, toaster, chairs, comic-strip creatures, ghosts, noses—and connect them with lines, a path of two lines, so that they all became the fruit of a single impossible tree. The exact age when this creative act so powerfully pleased me I cannot recall; the wish to make collections, to assemble sets, is surely a deep urge of the human mind in its playful, artistic aspect. As deep, it may be, as the urge to hear a story from beginning to end, or the little ecstasy of extracting resemblances from different things. Proust, of course, made simile the cornerstone of his theory of aesthetic bliss, and Plato, if I understand him right, felt that that which a set of subjects have in common *must* have a separate existence in itself, as the *idea* which delivers us, in our perception of the world, from the nightmare of nominalism. At any rate, to make a man of pencil and paper is as much a magical act as painting a bison with blood on the wall of a cave; a child, frail and overshadowed, and groping for his fate, herein *captures* something and, further, brings down praise from on high.

I have described the artistic transaction as being between the awakening ego and the world of matter to which it awakes; but no doubt the wish to please one's parents enters early, and remains with the artist all his life, as a desire to please the world, however displeasing his behavior may seem, and however self-satisfying the work pretends to be. We are surprised to discover, for instance, that Henry James hoped to make lots of money, and that James Joyce read all of his reviews. The artist's personality has an awkward ambivalence: he is a cave dweller who yet hopes to be pursued into his cave. The need for privacy, the need for recognition: a child's vulnerability speaks in both needs, and in my own reaction to, say, the beseeching mail just described, I detect the live ambiguity—one is avid to receive the letters, and loath to answer them. Or (to make reference to the literary scene I know best) consider the striking contrast between the eager, even breathless warmth of Saul Bellow's fiction, inviting our love and closeness with every phrase, and Bellow's own faintly haughty, distinctly edgy personal surface. Again, J. D. Salinger wrote a masterpiece, *The Catcher in the Rye,* recommending that readers who enjoy a book call up the author; then he spent his next twenty years avoiding the telephone. A writer, I would say, out of no doubt deficiencies of character, has constructed a cave-shaped organ, hollow more like a mouth than like an ear, through which he communicates with the world at one remove. Somewhat, perhaps, as his own subconscious communicates with him through dreams. Because the opportunities for feedback have been reduced to letters that need not be answered and telephones that can be unlisted, to an annual gauntlet of reviews and nonbestowal of prizes, the communication can be more honest than is any but the most trusting personal exchange; yet also great opportunities for distortion exist unchecked. For one more of these rather subterranean and reprehensible satisfactions of writing that I am here confessing is that the world, so balky and resistant and humiliating, can in the act of mimesis be rectified, adjusted, chastened, purified. Fantasies defeated in reality can be fully indulged; tendencies deflected by the cramp of circumstance can be followed to an end. In my own case I have noticed, so often it has ceased to surprise me, a prophetic quality of my fictions, even to the subsequent appearance in my life of originally fictional characters. We write, that is, out of latency as much as memory; and years later our laggard lives in reality act out, often with eerie fidelity, the patterns projected in our imaginings.

BUT WE HAVE COME too far, too fast, from that ambitious child making his pencil move beneath the stained-glass chandelier. In my adolescence I discovered one could write with a pencil as well as draw, without the annoying need to consult reality so frequently. Also, the cave beneath the written page holds many more kinds of space than the one beneath the drawing pad. My writing tends, I think, to be pictorial, not only in its groping for visual precision but in the way the books are conceived, as objects in space, with events and persons composed within them like shapes on a canvas. I do not recommend this approach; it is perhaps a perversion of the primal narrative urge. Storytelling, for all its powers of depiction, shares with music the medium of time, and perhaps its genius, its most central transformation, has to do with time, with rhythm and echo and the sense of time not frozen as in a painting but channeled and harnessed as in a symphony.

But one can give no more than what one has received, and we try to create for others, in our writings, aesthetic sensations we have experienced. In my case, some of these would be: the graphic precision of a Dürer or a Vermeer, the offhand-and-backwards-feeling verbal and psychological accuracy of a Henry Green, the wonderful embowering metaphors of Proust, the enigmatic concreteness of Kafka and Joyce, the collapse into components of a solved mathematical problem, the unriddling of a scrupulous mystery story, the earth-scorning scope of science fiction, the tear-producing results of a truly humorous piece of writing. Writing, really, can make us do rather few substantial things: it can make us laugh, it can make us weep, if it is pornography and we are young, it can make us come. It can also, of course, make us sleep; and though in the frequent discussion of the writer's social purpose this soporific effect is unfailingly ignored, I suspect it is the most widespread practical effect of writing—a book is less often a flaming sword or a beam of light than a bedtime toddy. Whatever the use, we hope that some members of society will find our product useful enough to purchase; but I think it would be a hypocrisy to pretend that these other people's welfare, or communication with them, or desire to ennoble or radicalize or terrify or lull them, is the primary reason why one writes.

No, what a writer wants, as every aspiring writer

can tell you, is to *get into print*. To transform the changing shadows of one's dimly and fitfully lived life into print—into metal or, with the advent of offset printing, into rather mysteriously electrified rubber—to lift through the doubled magic of language and mechanical reproduction our own impressions and dreams and playful constructions into another realm of existence, a multiplied and far-flung existence, into space far wider than that which we occupy, into a time theoretically eternal: *that* is the siren song that holds us to our desks, our dismal revisions, our insomnia panics, our dictionaries and encyclopedias, our lonely and, the odds long are, superfluous labor. "Of making many books there is no end; and much study is a weariness of the flesh." A weariness one can certainly feel entering even a modestly well-stocked bookstore. Yet it is just this involvement in the world of commerce and industry, this imposition of one's otherwise evanescent fancies upon the machinery of manufacture and distribution, that excites the writer's ego, and gives an illusion of triumph over his finitude.

Although, as a child, I lived what was to become my material and message, my wish to write did not begin with that material and message; rather, it was a wish to escape from it, into an altogether better world. When I was thirteen, a magazine came into the house, *The New Yorker* by name, and I loved that magazine so much I concentrated all my wishing into an effort to make myself small and inky and intense enough to be received into its pages. Once there, I imagined, some transfigured mode of being, called a "writer's life," would begin for me. My fantasy was not entirely fantastic, as my domineering position on this platform and the first-class airplane tickets that brought me halfway around the world testify. But what I would not altogether insincerely ask you to accept is something shabby, precarious, and even craven about a writer's life.

Among artists, a writer's equipment is least out of reach—the language we all more or less use, a little patience at grammar and spelling, the common adventures of blundering mortals. A painter must learn to paint; his studio is redolent of alchemic substances and physical force. The musician's arcanum of specialized knowledge and personal dexterity is even more intimidating, less accessible to the untrained, and therefore somehow less corruptible than the writer's craft. Though some painters and musicians go bad in the prime of their lives, far fewer do, and few so drastically, as writers. Our trick is treacherously thin; our art is so incorrigibly amateur, that novices constantly set the world of letters on its ear, and the very phrase "professional writer" has a grimy sound. Hilaire Belloc said that the trouble with writing was that it was never meant to be a profession, it was meant to be a hobby. An act of willful play, as I have described it.

So I have not spoken up to now of language, of

the joys of using it well, of the role of the writer as a keeper of the keys of language, a guardian of usage and enforcer of precision. This does not seem to me a very real notion, however often it is put forward. Language goes on evolving in the street and in the spoken media, and well-written books are the last places it looks for direction. The writer follows after the spoken language, usually timidly. I see myself described in reviews as a doter upon words. It is true, I am grateful to have been born into English, with its polyglot flexibility and the happy accident, in the wake of two empires, of its worldwide currency. But what I am conscious of doting on is not English *per se,* its pliable grammar and abundant synonyms, but its potential, for the space of some phrases or paragraphs, of becoming reality, of engendering out of imitation another reality, infinitely lesser but thoroughly possessed, thoroughly human.

Pascal says, "When a natural discourse paints a passion or an effect, one feels within oneself the truth of what one reads, which was there before, although one did not know it. Hence one is inclined to love him who makes us feel it, for he has not shown us his own riches, but ours." The writer's strength is not his own; he is a conduit who so positions himself that the world at his back flows through to the readers on the other side of the page. To keep this conduit scoured is his laborious task; to be, in the act of writing, anonymous, the end of his quest for fame.

. . . .

BEGINNING, THEN, WITH CUNNING private ambitions and a childish fascination with the implements of graphic representation, I find myself arrived, in this audible search for self-justification, at an embarrassed altruism. Beginning with the wish to make an impression, one ends wishing to erase the impression, to make of it a perfect transparency, to make of oneself a point of focus purely, as selfless as a lens. One begins by seeking celebrity and ends by feeling a terrible impatience with everything—every flattering attention, every invitation to speak and to impersonate a wise man, every hunger of the ego and of the body—an impatience with everything that clouds and clots our rapt witness to the world that surrounds and transcends us. A writer begins with his personal truth, with that obscure but vulnerable and, once lost, precious life that he lived before becoming a writer; but, those first impressions discharged—a process of years—he finds himself, though empty, still posed in the role of a writer, with it may be an expectant audience of sorts and certainly a habit of communion. It is then that he dies as a writer, and becomes an inert cultural object merely, or is born again, by resubmitting his ego, as it were, to fresh drafts of experience and refined operations of his mind. *To remain interested*—of American novelists, only Henry James continued in old age to advance his art; most, indeed, wrote their best novels first, or virtually first. Energy ebbs as we live; success breeds disillusion as surely as failure; the power of hope to generate action and vision lessens. Almost alone the writer can reap profit from this loss. An opportunity to sing louder from within the slackening ego is his. For his song has never been all his own: he has been its excuse as much as its source. The little tyrant's delight in wielding a pencil always carried with it an empathy into the condition of *being* a pencil; more and more the writer thinks of himself as an instrument, a means whereby a time and a place make their mark. To become less and transmit more, to replenish energy with wisdom—some such hope, at this more than midpoint of my life, is the reason why I write.

3

Writing in the Dark
David Grossman
Translated by Jessica Cohen

"Our personal happiness or unhappiness, our 'terrestrial' condition, is of great importance for the things we write," says Natalia Ginzburg in *It's Hard to Talk About Yourself,* in a chapter in which she discusses her life and writing after a deep personal tragedy.

It is hard to talk about yourself, and so before I reflect on my writing experience now, at this time in my life, let me say a few words about the effects of a trauma, a disaster situation, on a society and on a nation as a whole.

The words of the mouse from Kafka's short story "A Little Fable" come to mind. As the trap closes in on the mouse and the cat prowls beyond, he says,

"Alas, the world is growing smaller every day." After many years of living in an extreme and violent state of political, military, and religious conflict, I am sad to report that Kafka's mouse was right: the world is indeed growing smaller, growing narrower, every day. I can also tell you about the void that slowly emerges between the individual and the violent, chaotic state that encompasses practically every aspect of his life.

This void does not remain empty. It quickly fills up with apathy, cynicism, and above all despair—the despair that can fuel a distorted reality for many years, sometimes generations. The despair that one will never manage to change the situation, never redeem it. And the deepest despair of all—the despair of human beings, of what the distorted situation ultimately exposes in each of us.

I feel the heavy price that I and the people around me pay for this prolonged state of war. Part of this price is a shrinking of our soul's surface area—those parts of us that touch the violent, menacing world outside—and a diminished ability and willingness to empathize at all with other people in pain. We also pay the price by suspending our moral judgment, and we give up on understanding what we ourselves think. Given a situation so frightening, so deceptive, and so complicated—both morally and practically—we feel it may be better not to think or know. Better to hand over the job of thinking and doing and setting moral standards to those who are surely "in the know." Better not to feel too much until the crisis ends—and if it never ends, at least we'll have suffered a little less, developed a useful dullness, protected ourselves as much as we could with a little indifference, a little repression, a little deliberate blindness, and a large dose of self-anesthetics.

The constant—and very real—fear of being hurt, the fear of death, of intolerable loss, or even of "mere" humiliation, leads each of us, the citizens and prisoners of the conflict, to dampen our own vitality, our emotional and intellectual range, and to cloak ourselves in more and more protective layers until we suffocate.

Kafka's mouse was right: when your predator closes in on you, your world does get smaller. So does the language that describes it.

From experience I can say that the language used by the citizens of a conflict to describe their situation becomes flatter and flatter as the conflict goes on, gradually evolving into a series of clichés and slogans. It starts with the jargon invented by the systems that handle the conflict directly—the army, the police, the bureaucracy. The trend spreads into the mass media, which create an elaborate, shrewd language designed to tell their audiences the most palatable story (thereby erecting a barrier between everything the state does in the twilight zone of the conflict and the way its citizens choose to see themselves). The process eventually seeps into the private, intimate language of the citizens (even if they vehemently deny it).

The evolution is all too understandable: human language's natural richness and its ability to touch on the finest nuances of existence can be truly hurtful in a state of conflict because they constantly remind us of the exuberant reality that we have lost, of its complexities and subtleties. The more hopeless the situation seems and the shallower the language becomes, the more public discourse dwindles, until all that remains are tired recriminations between the enemies or between political adversaries within the state. All that remains are the clichés we use to describe the enemy and ourselves—the prejudices, mythological anxieties, and crude generalizations with which we trap ourselves and ensnare our enemies. The world indeed grows smaller.

These thoughts are relevant not only to the conflict in the Middle East. In so many parts of the world today billions of people face some threat to the existence, the values, the liberty, and the identity of human beings. Almost every one of us faces his own threat, his own curse. Each of us feels—or can guess—how his unique "situation" may quickly become a trap that will rob his freedom, his sense of home in his country, his private language, his free will.

In this reality, we authors and poets write. In Israel and in Palestine, in Chechnya and in Sudan, in New York and in the Congo. There are times in my workday, after a few hours of writing, when I look up and think: Now, at this very moment, sits another author, whom I do not know, in Damascus or Tehran, in

Kigali or Dublin, who, like me, is engaged in the strange, baseless, wonderful work of creation, within a reality that contains so much violence and alienation, indifference and diminishment. I have a distant ally who does not know me, and together we are weaving this shapeless web, which nonetheless has immense power, the power to change a world and create a world, the power to give words to the mute and to bring about *tikkun*—"repair"—in the deepest, kabbalistic sense of the word.

As FOR MYSELF, IN the works of fiction I have written in recent years, I have almost intentionally turned my back on the immediate, burning reality of my country, the reality of the latest news bulletin. I have written books about this reality in the past, and I have never stopped discussing it and trying to understand it through essays, articles, and interviews. I have taken part in dozens of protests and international peace initiatives. I have met with my neighbors—some of whom were my enemies— every time I thought there was any chance for dialogue. Yet over the past few years, out of a decision that is almost a protest, I have not written about these disaster zones in my *literature*.

Why? Because I wanted to write about other things, things no less important, things for which it's hard to find the time, the emotion, and the total at-

tention, while the near-eternal war thunders on outside. I wrote about a husband's obsessive jealousy of his wife, about homeless children on the streets of Jerusalem, about a man and a woman who establish a private, almost hermetic language within their reverie of love. I wrote about the loneliness of Samson, the biblical hero, I wrote about the subtle and tangled relationships between women and their mothers, and between children and parents in general.

Roughly four years ago, when my second son was about to enlist in the army, I could no longer remain where I was. I was overcome with an almost physical sense of urgency and alarm that gave me no rest. I began then to write a novel that deals directly with the difficult reality I live in, a novel that describes how the cruelty of the external situation invades the delicate, intimate fabric of one family, ultimately tearing it to shreds.

"At the moment someone is writing," says Natalia Ginzburg, "he is miraculously driven to forget the immediate circumstances of his own life. . . . But whether we are happy or unhappy leads us to write in one way or another. When we are happy our imagination is stronger; when we are unhappy our memory works with greater vitality."

It is hard to talk about yourself. I will only say what I can say at this time, from where I stand now.

I write. The consciousness of the disaster that befell me upon the death of my son Uri in the Second

Lebanon War now permeates every minute of my life. The power of memory is indeed great and heavy, and at times has a paralyzing effect. Nevertheless, the act of writing creates for me a "space" of sorts, an emotional expanse that I have never known before, where death is more than the absolute, unambiguous opposite of life.

The authors who are here today know: when we write, we feel the world in flux, elastic, full of possibilities—unfrozen. Anywhere the human element exists, there is no freezing and no paralysis, and there is no status quo (even if we sometimes mistakenly think there is; even if there are those who would very much like us to think there is).

I write, and the world does not close in on me. It does not grow smaller. It moves in the direction of what is open, future, possible.

I imagine, and the act of imagination revives me. I am not fossilized or paralyzed in the face of predators. I invent characters. Sometimes I feel as if I am digging people out of the ice in which reality has encased them. But perhaps, more than anything, the person I am digging out at the moment is myself.

I write. I feel the many possibilities that exist in every human situation, and I feel my capacity to choose among them. I feel the sweetness of liberty, which I thought I had lost. I take pleasure in the richness of a real, personal, intimate language. I remember the delights of breathing fully, properly, when I manage to escape the claustrophobia of slogans and clichés. I begin to breathe with both lungs.

I write, and I feel that the correct and accurate use of words acts like a medicine. It purifies the air I breathe, removes the pollutants, and frustrates the schemes of language defrauders and language rapists. I write and feel my sensitivity to language and my intimacy with its different layers, with its sensuality and humor, restore me to myself, to the person I was before my selfhood was expropriated by the conflict, by the governments and the armies, by the despair and the tragedy.

I write. I purge myself of one of the dubious but typical talents that arise in a state of war—the talent for being an enemy, nothing but an enemy. I write, and I try not to shield myself from the legitimacy and the suffering of my enemy, or from the tragedy and the complexity of his life, or from his mistakes and crimes, or from knowing what I myself am doing to him. Nor do I shelter myself from the surprising similarities I discover between him and me.

I write. And all at once I am no longer doomed to face this absolute, false, suffocating dichotomy— this inhuman choice between "victim" and "aggressor," without any third, more human option. When I write, I can be a whole person, with natural passages between my various parts, and with some parts that feel close to the suffering and the just assertions of my enemies without giving up my own identity at all.

At times, in the course of writing, I can remember what we all felt in Israel for one rare moment, when Egyptian president Anwar Sadat's plane landed in Tel Aviv after decades of war between the two nations. We suddenly discovered how heavy the burden was that we had been carrying all our lives—the burden of hostility and fear and suspicion. The burden of having to always be on guard, to always be an enemy, all the time. How blissful it was in that moment to do away with the massive armor of suspicion, hatred, and prejudice. How frighteningly blissful it was to stand naked, to stand pure, and watch as before our eyes a human face emerged from the narrow, one-dimensional depiction we had been seeing for years.

I write, and I give my most private and intimate names to an external, unknown world. In some sense, I make it mine. So do I return from a land of exile and alienation—I come home. I change, just slightly, what previously seemed unchangeable. Even when I describe the cruelest arbitrariness that determines my fate—whether man-made or preordained—I suddenly find in it new subtleties and nuances. I find that simply writing about the arbitrariness lets me move freely in its presence. That the very fact of standing up against the arbitrariness gives me freedom— perhaps the only freedom man has against any kind of arbitrariness—the freedom to articulate the tragedy of my situation *in my own words*. The freedom to articulate myself differently, freshly, against the unbending dictates of arbitrariness that threaten to bind me and pin me down.

I also write about what cannot be restored. About what has no comfort. Then too, in a way I still cannot explain, the circumstances of my life do not close in on me and leave me paralyzed. Many times a day, as I sit at my writing desk, I touch sorrow and loss like someone touching electricity with bare hands, yet it does not kill me. I do not understand how this miracle has come to pass. Perhaps after I finish this novel, I will try to understand. Not now. It is too soon.

I write the life of my country, Israel. A tortured country, drugged to the point of overdose by history, by emotions beyond what humans can contain, by an extreme excess of events and tragedy, by an excess of fear and a crippling sobriety, by an excess of memory, by dashed hopes, by a fate unique among nations. It is an existence that sometimes seems to take on the proportions of a mythic tale, diminishing our prospects of ever living an ordinary life as a state.

We authors know periods of despair and self-loathing. Our work, fundamentally, entails dismantling personalities and relinquishing some of our most effective defense mechanisms. Willingly we struggle with the hardest, ugliest, rawest, and most painful matters of the soul. Our work forces us, again and again, to acknowledge our helplessness as people and as artists.

Yet still—and this is the great miracle, the alchemy

of our act—in some sense, from the moment we take pen in hand or put fingers to keyboard, we have already ceased to be a victim at the mercy of all that enslaved and restricted us before we began writing.

We write. How fortunate we are: The world does not close in on us. The world does not grow smaller.

4

Out from Under the Cloud of Unknowing
Francine Prose

1. Why I'm Not Writing the Essay I Was Going to Write.
I'd planned to read or reread some of the novels that
were widely read and discussed during the height of
the seventies feminist movement, a historical moment
when women were not only burning their bras and
demonstrating outside the Miss America pageant but
suddenly paying attention to all sorts of things that
for some inexplicable reason they'd never registered
before. How *could* we not have noticed that we were
doing all the housework and raising the kids and not
getting any credit, and that, when we went to work,
we were getting paid a fraction of what the equally
alienated and not so equally underpaid guy in the
next cubicle was getting? Or (more relevantly in my
case, since, in my youth of boho squalor, I never did

housework and had no kids and only *wished* I could get a job and be underpaid) it began to seem amazing how often it was assumed that having a vagina automatically meant I was less intelligent, talented, capable, and interesting than the world's least interesting human being who happened to have a penis.

Looking back, now that all of that is settled and everything's fifty-fifty between women and men, salaries included, you might think that these little glitches of gender inequality would always have been obvious—but trust me, it was a revelation. And as so often happens when the system is dealt a shock, after-tremors (or in some cases, pre-tremors) reverberated through literature and art.

Obviously, there were artists who realized all along that there were some . . . well, *drawbacks* to ordinary female existence. Flaubert got it right, as did Ibsen, Charlotte Brontë, Virginia Woolf, and so many others.

Then in the seventies and early eighties, other novels began appearing, semi-literary, semi–something else—Erica Jong's *Fear of Flying,* Marilyn French's *The Women's Room,* novels with sandboxes and mad housewives in their titles—that women took to heart. They discovered themselves in the characters: the so-called liberated woman coping with a sexual double standard, the housewife learning that she has an actual brain in which her husband and kids have minimal or no interest.

My idea was to read some of them and then

read some contemporary novels marketed to young women and see . . . I don't know what I thought I would see. What had changed and what hadn't.

This idea lasted thirty or forty pages into each book in a stack of books. Each time, I found myself putting down the novel and wondering what was in the refrigerator. Maybe I *hadn't* seen that *Law & Order* rerun I was pretty sure I'd seen.

Life was short. I just couldn't do it. I couldn't face the prospect of not being particularly entertained and instead spending hundreds or thousands of pages being told more or less what I've just said about gender inequality in a couple of paragraphs.

2. What This Made Me Think Of.

At the risk of sounding even more like a gender traitor . . . The morning after I scrapped the idea of the essay I planned to write, I found myself wondering why so much feminist visual art of the same period seemed, in retrospect, so crappy and reductive. I was thinking in particular of works such as Judy Chicago's *The Dinner Party,* a piece which invites the viewer to a monumental formal dinner with a pantheon of female geniuses or, more specifically, to dine (visually and metaphorically) with their genitalia, on plates. I also had in mind the artists whose paintings, sculptures, and installations took off from the inarguably true observation that traditional "women's work"— quilting, beading, embroidery, and so forth—has always been undervalued. But at this point, frankly,

I'd much rather have the quilts, the beadwork, and the embroidery than the art these "crafts" inspired.

In fact all sorts of worthwhile causes have spawned work that unintentionally suggests that art needs to do something beyond calling your attention to a problem, or stating a good idea you've probably already had. To work from this sort of constricted and controlling perspective makes art seem yanked and jerked around to fit a strange and artificial armature; in fiction, the world we are reading about seems at once too much and not enough like the world we know. Chekhov warned about the problem of trying to combine a work of art and a sermon. He claimed it was a problem of brevity, or economy, but he was being partly ironic, as he often was in his letters.

3. What to Do Instead?

Practically anything. Countless masterpieces have a strong political element. Certain of Caravaggio's paintings will tell you everything you need to know about the human thirst for violence and blood, which is, I would say, a political subject. Spend some time looking at Manet's *The Execution of the Emperor Maximilian.* Shakespeare's history plays, as well as *Macbeth* and *Julius Caesar,* are nothing if not political. *Anna Karenina* is a feminist tract written by a man who believed that most women were shallow, manipulative, and weak—deeply inferior creatures. George Eliot was brilliant at describing the processes by which decisions are arrived at, another political subject. I've been trying to recall the name of a novel in which one character tells another to read *The Red and the Black* because it's a political novel. Practically a spy novel.

There are dozens of astonishing political memoirs. Nadezhda Mandelstam's *Hope Against Hope,* Mihail Sebastian's *Journal 1935–1944, The Diary of Anne Frank.* And politics can slip its way into poetry in a way that's serious, graceful, and sly. The Eastern Europeans have a historical jump on the necessity that pressured Szymborska and Herbert to find the perfect metaphor or elliptical narrative with which to talk about, or more often *around*, their historical moment.

Other possible end runs around the difficulty of so-called political art include making the protagonist not the good guy but the bad one, not smart old compassionate sensible *us,* but the clueless or compromised Other. Like the complex, educated, intermittently charming and thuggish Jack in Wallace Shawn's *The Designated Mourner.* Or the substance-addled, God-haunted expats in the novels of Robert Stone. Or the spacey, self-involved gringo Gullivers unable to see the realities of Central American life in Deborah Eisenberg's *Under the 82nd Airborne.* Or the brilliantly drawn William Houston in Denis Johnson's *Tree of Smoke,* who in the novel's first pages blows away a monkey for no particular reason aside from alcohol and the Vietnam War. Or the careerist, Pinochet-enabling priest in Roberto Bolaño's *By Night in Chile.*

4. Full Disclosure.

Of the five writers I mentioned in the paragraph above, two are close friends, two are acquaintances of whom I'm fond. I wish I'd known Roberto Bolaño. I say this as a disclaimer for the benefit of those who appear to believe writers are all a bunch of sleazy grifters conspiring to hype their pals' work and boost their friends' careers. I guess I should also say that the story I am about to mention was written by a former student. That I feel compelled to make these disclosures seems to me indicative of a political climate in which we are encouraged to suspect and simultaneously venerate and despise anyone who makes any contribution to our culture, however large or small, meretricious or well-intentioned.

5. A Great Political Story.

ZZ Packer's story "Brownies" has, as its center, an African-American brownie troop at summer camp. There has rarely been a more incisive picture of how power gets tossed around in a group, here a group of little girls. Race reveals itself as an issue, as a social hierarchy with a remarkably subtle and complicated architecture that is only revealed to us as the plot keeps turning.

Another great political story is Mavis Gallant's "Mlle. Dias de Corta," a first-person (second-person, actually) cry from the heart in the voice of an old woman, calling out to her eponymous former tenant with whom she has had a (to say the least) complicated history, which the story tells. Among the many things we learn about this old woman is that she is a French nationalist, and by the end of the story we understand (among many things) why someone like this woman (not that there's anyone *like* this woman) might be one.

6. Is Beckett's Work Political?

Why else have his plays proved so popular with prisoners and with citizens of besieged Balkan capitals?

7. A Quote from Grace Paley.

Here's a quote from Grace Paley, who *liked* to be called political. It's from an essay in a book I've had for probably thirty years, a collection entitled *Writers as Teachers/Teachers as Writers,* edited by Jonathan Baumbach and published in 1970. The quote concerns politics and literature, though you'll notice that Grace Paley uses neither of those words.

> It's possible to write about anything in the world, but the slightest story ought to contain the facts of money and blood in order to be interesting to adults. That is—everybody continues on this earth by courtesy of certain economic arrangements, people are rich or poor, make a living or don't have to, are useful to systems, or superfluous. —And blood—the way people live as families or outside families or in the creation of family, sisters, sons, fathers, the bloody ties.

8. Is There Money and Blood in Calvino?

In *The Baron in the Trees,* the boy who goes up in the trees and never comes down is not only *a baron* but the narrator's *brother.*

9. More Money, More Blood.

At the moment, one of my favorite stories is Bolaño's "Mauricio ('The Eye') Silva." I suppose I could say it's about a photographer whom the narrator knows from Mexico City and whom he meets years later, by which point the photographer has an extremely strange story to tell him. I could say that everything that happens in the story is informed by politics, but in a way that is so mysterious that to explain what I mean would require summarizing every single thing that happens in the story. Which is all completely mysterious. You might as well read the story.

10. Maybe the Best Political Writing
Is the Most Mysterious.

Maybe that is the problem that politics has with art. It's the problem of mystery, which politics (con-structed in a narrow sense) doesn't like, or, perhaps more accurately, doesn't feel comfortable with. Like science, politics would sooner find an explanation, or an entire system.

Maybe that was the trouble with the novels I tried to read: They were insufficiently mysterious. A led to B, which led directly to C without a skip or side step into something more unexpected—in narrative, character, or language. The polemicist, or the theorist, or the strategist would have trouble with the stance that Chekhov identified as basic for the artist. That is, the notion that writers must admit they understand nothing of life, that nothing in this world makes sense, so all a writer can do is to try and describe it.

Maybe, like other arts, political art might as well start from there—not from the impulse to teach or inform, but from the desire to discover and grope our way out from under what a fourteenth-century English monk called the cloud of unknowing.

5

The Man, the Men at the Station
Pico Iyer

got off the overnight train in Mandalay, Burma's historical city of kings, and instantly there was a swarm of men around me. They were hard for me to tell apart, most of them, dressed in white shirts, with wraparound *longyis* around their waists, many of them wild-eyed and unshaven after spending all night in their trishaws. Like people in many countries that I'd seen, they were at once trying to arrest my attention and to avoid the attention of all the passersby or seeming passengers (or even fellow trishaw drivers) who might be making a living by giving names to the police. How to stand out, how to get by, and yet how not to attract notice: it is one of the never-ending predicaments in a country such as Burma.

I settled at last on one of them, with a straggly

beard and rough, rural features, and we bargained a little on the street. Maung-Maung, as he asked me to call him, had a sign on one side of his half-broken little vehicle, "My Life," and a sign on the other, "B.Sc. Mathematics." I could tell that, like many of his fellows, he was bright, resourceful, well-educated, but in Burma intelligence (in all senses) is something to be feared and can best be used by giving oneself to something other than words and ideas. I felt something of the unease that many a traveler feels in such a setting: it was as if I, through no gift of my own, had stepped down off the movie screen that Maung-Maung and his friends had been watching for most of their lives— an emissary from a land of freedom, possibility, and movement—and now they were reaching for me as if I could carry them back to my make-believe world.

We got into his little trishaw at last, I in the throne at the back, and he pedaling furiously, to show me the sights. After a short while, though, he turned off the main boulevard and we started entering unscripted land: the houses grew smaller and smaller, more entangled in undergrowth, and the bustle fell away, so that I felt I was being taken into a kind of underworld. My new friend sensed, perhaps, the stiffening in me, and so he passed back a small piece of jade, as he cycled, and told me that it was a present, for me. A present from the citizen of a desperately poor country to a visitor from the world's richest? It sounded strange. Then he passed back something even more valuable: a photo album with its protagonists carefully marked out. "My Monk." "My Headmaster." "My Brothers and Sisters."

I took all this in, and then a final book came my way, in which my new friend had written out his precepts for living: he would always abstain from the toxins of life, he had written, and try to show kindness. Those were the guidelines his monk had drawn for him, he said.

I didn't know where we were going and whom I was ending up with as he cycled, steadily, into rougher and rougher parts of town—this is the traveler's predicament, perhaps his excitement—and when we came at last to a tiny hut, weeds growing all around it, I wasn't sure at all whether I wanted to go in. This wasn't listed in any guidebook I had seen. Still, I followed Maung-Maung into his home and sat on the bed that his roommate used at night (a trishaw driver in Burma cannot afford to live alone). Slowly, as if he were pulling out what was true contraband, my friend reached under his bed and drew out his treasures.

A sociology textbook: *Life in Modern America*. A faded Burmese-English dictionary, out of which he had copied sentences: *"If you do this, you may end up in jail." "My heart is lacerated by what you said."* A book of photos of the foreigners he had met, their arms around him, the faraway places they belonged to implicit in the cameras around their necks, the excited gleam in their eyes.

Until two years ago, Maung-Maung told me, he had never met anyone from outside Burma. "Only in movies." In villages like his own, in the Shan States, people with opportunities might as well belong to another planet. Then he showed me the place in the album in which he had pasted every letter he had ever received from abroad. We sat in the little room on the hot autumn day and looked at stamps and messages from California and Paris and Australia.

I suppose I had been in rooms like this many times already—in Tibet and Colombia and Egypt. Soon it would seem as if most of my life was being spent with people like Maung-Maung, who represent the majority of our global neighbors. But still I had never met someone quite like this. He passed across an essay—"My Life," it was titled, as the sign on his trishaw was—and I read of how he had grown up with parents who could never imagine an education for themselves. They had despaired when their eldest son went off to the city— and then had shaken their heads when he took to digging holes for a living, and washing clothes in a monastery. When they heard he had become a trishaw driver, usually sleeping in his vehicle, they never wanted to hear another word, imagining the lowlifes and street girls who must be his companions now.

Still, Maung-Maung told me, he dreamed of the day when he would buy an English suit and invite his old parents to his graduation, as he received a "Further Certificate" in mathematics. Possibilities were scant in brutally oppressed Burma, and since the government had closed every door and locked every window, all that remained were such imaginings.

. . . .

AND, I BEGAN TO suppose, people like me. I added to Maung-Maung's collection of addresses and photographs, and after I returned to California, I often heard from him, just as I heard from other Maung-Maungs I had recently met in China, the Philippines, Nepal. Every few weeks, so it seemed, a worn blue envelope would arrive, with his looping script—"Maung-Maung, Trishaw Stand, Mandalay, Burma"—on the back, and stamps that must have cost a day's wages or more to buy, even when the letters were smuggled out through foreigners traveling to Thailand.

He was still at his trishaw stand, my friend wrote, in carefully inscribed English (I thought of the dictionary, the almost lightless room from which they came); he still hoped to become a teacher of mathematics. "Sometimes I don't even get one kyat for a day," Maung-Maung wrote. "Anyhow, I will try to improve for my living and I will support to my old parents. I have to try for success, then happiness. But I don't want to wish for what is impossible."

He never asked me for money or presents or support for a visa; he asked only that I never mention politics in my letters, and that I remember how often letters got intercepted and devoured by the wrong eyes. I followed every precaution, but still, at some point, I realized that the letters had stopped. I shuddered to think what might happen to a curious and intellectually engaged man in Burma, where the government was fearful of everything and ruled on astrological whimsy, at one point outlawing all currency notes in denominations of 10 and 5—because 9 was a more auspicious number—and thus effectively robbing the people of all their savings.

I scheduled a trip to go back to the country, partly to see my friend again. But one day after they issued my visa, the consular officials at the Burmese embassy in Tokyo happened to see my photo in *Time* magazine, realized I was a journalist, and called me up to ask if I would mind if they canceled the visa (since the alternative was going to Burma and being arrested on the spot, I accepted). That same month, demonstrations broke out in the capital and three thousand people or more were killed.

THIS IS A STORY that every traveler will recognize; I would come to know it by heart as I traveled to North Korea and Ethiopia and Laos and Haiti. Words cannot easily do justice to the lives that crowd in on one in most countries in the world, and ask why they shouldn't receive an answer. Burma, after the demonstrations, became Myanmar, even farther from the notice of the world; occasionally it would slip into the news, as a factor in some geopolitical equation, but for most of us it disappeared entirely behind a curtain, just as its government hoped it would. Of the government, indeed, we heard now and then; of the people, cloudless, good-natured, and as sweet and kind as any I had met on my travels, we never heard at all.

"How can you go to a country where your very presence there counts as a vote of confidence in its oppressors?" friends sometimes asked me. "Every penny you spend goes towards the oppression." It was never an easy question to answer, but when I thought of Maung-Maung, and all his neighbors, I imagined that if they were asked, they would nearly always vote for our presence. Without us, they were essentially condemned to solitary confinement for life.

The years passed, and I thought constantly of Maung-Maung, and his unmet neighbors in Yemen and Cuba and Bolivia. Occasionally, friends would head off to Mandalay, but after 1988 none of them reported meeting my friend. Then, fourteen years after our meeting, I received a letter, from an un-known address in London, saying that the sender had met someone I knew in Myanmar—he recognized him because he'd read about him in a book I'd writ-ten—and had a letter he wanted to pass on.

I waited anxiously, and nothing came.

Then, a few months later, another envelope ar-rived, from Montreal, and when I opened it up, the familiar handwriting tumbled out. "Dear Pico Iyer," Maung-Maung wrote, and told me of how, not long after we met, he had met some other visistors, from Texas. This elderly couple had been so moved by my friend—his essay "My Life," the presents he bestowed on them—that they had decided, then and there, to give him two hundred dollars, to realize his lifelong dream of buying his own trishaw. He could not believe his good karma, and he had gone home to his wife and five children and told them that now their lives would be transformed. Even his parents, he thought, might hold him in higher regard now.

Then, Maung-Maung wrote, he met another visitor, from Italy, who was so moved by his story that he had promised to give him the money to realize his secret wish, the one he had confided to almost nobody, of buying a camera and becoming a photographer. "Just get me some old coins," the visitor had said, "and I'll give you a camera in return."

Maung-Maung raced around Mandalay, emptying his savings to acquire old Burmese coins, and sent them to the Italian. But when he traveled across Burma to the capital, and waited at the appointed place to receive his camera, nobody showed up. He waited and waited, and then traveled home and told his wife that they were broken. They would have to return to their village in shame and start the whole process again.

It was twelve years since that moment, Maung-Maung wrote, and at last, through hard work and determination, he had got back to where he started. He was a trishaw driver again, sleeping in his vehicle outside the station in Mandalay, and he looked forward to my return. He was too old now to expect further certificates or graduation ceremonies, but at least we might meet again one day. I'd written about him in a book, he knew, so there were others now who knew of the details of "My Life."

I didn't have the heart to tell him that I was on a blacklist in Burma, perhaps because of writing about people like himself, suitably disguised. A colleague had seen my picture up at the airport, as a criminal to be arrested if ever he showed his face. The important thing was that we had contact at last, and a window, a tiny window, had opened again where before there had seemed no hope.

It's almost a quarter of a century now since our paths crossed, but I think of Maung-Maung often, especially when I meet the other Maung-Maungs who become the protagonists of a traveler's life. Sometimes it seems that my mailbox is mostly full of their letters (people like Maung-Maung have incentive to write, and the Internet is all but banned in such countries). I walk down the street outside my apartment in rural Japan, and send a letter back, or buy a book about their country, or even write a piece like this. Every one of those simple acts is impossible for them. The things I take for granted are the stuff of science-fiction fantasy for most.

For all the derelictions and brutalities of his government, though, Maung-Maung is still waiting at the station, and we are the only freedom he knows. Without us—the stories we take to him, the stories we bring back from him—there wouldn't be anything, except years and years of further struggle, and then nothing at all.

6

Notes on Literature and Engagement
Russell Banks

ovelists, story writers, and poets have nearly always positioned themselves in support of justice, human rights, and equality. As individuals, that is. As citizens of a particular nation or even of the world. And why not? For who would position himself *against* justice, human rights, and equality? It's an easy vote to cast, no matter what your political party or ideology or religion happens to be.

And on those occasions when literary men and women have taken up their pens as journalists and essayists, whether their personal politics are of the right, center, or left, they have inevitably written in defense of humanity against the forces of . . . well, the forces of *inhumanity*. In general, this is true also of philosophers and scientists, of musicians, of academics, of social scientists, and so on—the so-called intelligentsia—when they speak out as individuals. This is not surprising, nor should it be.

But a work of literature is not a vote, and a novelist writing (I speak here mainly of novelists, because I am one) is not a voter or even, for that matter, a citizen of a particular nation or of the world. A novelist is not an essayist or a journalist, either. Not when he or she is writing novels. And he is certainly not a politician. Nor is he a political activist working for change, writing fiction in *support* of a policy or set of policies or of candidates for office.

A novelist writing is simply a person sitting alone in a room with his sentences, composing them by the thousands one at a time, learning from each new sentence that he or she writes what the next sentence will be. The fact is, the novelist speaks for no one but himself or herself and writes solely to penetrate what would otherwise remain mysterious to him, morally or metaphysically or socially. Mysterious and impenetrable—except by means of the silent, solitary act of writing a novel, this novel, the one at hand. And the very same conditions will prevail when, after finishing this novel, he or she sits down at the desk and begins to write another.

Perhaps this is why, in the nearly three-hundred-year history of American literature, so very few novels have managed to be significant forces for social change. You can count them on one hand. Perhaps the most famous of the American novels that actu-

NOTES ON LITERATURE AND ENGAGEMENT

ally had an effect on government policy are Upton
Sinclair's *The Jungle*, published in 1906, which ex-
posed the horrors of the meatpacking industry, leading to the passage of the Meat Inspection Act and the
Pure Food and Drug Act of 1906 and the creation of
the Food and Drug Administration; and *Uncle Tom's
Cabin* by Harriet Beecher Stowe, published in 1852,
a runaway best seller that electrified the antislavery
movement and brought into the Abolitionist fold
thousands of decent white Americans who, until they
read her novel, had not known where they stood on
the greatest moral question we Americans have had
to face.

When, towards the end of the Civil War, Stowe
was introduced at the White House to President Lin-
coln, he said, "So this is the little lady who made this
big war." Which was not exactly true, of course, as
she did not wish for war, merely desired the end of
slavery, but her novel certainly *helped* start it. When
The Jungle was published it, too, was an instant best
seller and was championed by an American president, Theodore Roosevelt, who responded to pres-
sure from the meat producers themselves. They were
actually pushing for regulation. The novel was such
a sensation that foreign and domestic sales of American meat had fallen by one-half, and the only way
the meatpacking companies could get their market
share back was to have the federal government, at
taxpayers' expense, guarantee the cleanliness of the
product.

Sinclair's ambition for his novel, however, was to improve the living conditions and wages of the workers, all workers, and to expose the cruel effects of laissez-faire capitalism on the poor. The title, *The Jungle,* is an allusion to a Hobbesian universe ruled by survival of the fittest. Sinclair said, "I aimed at the public's heart, and by accident I hit it in the stomach." When he first arrived at the Chicago stockyards to begin his research, he is supposed to have announced, "Hello, I'm Upton Sinclair, and I'm here to write the *Uncle Tom's Cabin* of the Labor Movement!"

Uncle Tom's Cabin is a mawkish melodrama. Because we all now know where we stand on the question of slavery, it is not much read today, except in high schools and colleges, usually as part of the curriculum concerned with the Abolitionist movement and the causes of the Civil War. It's not read as literature, as a work of art. Probably it never was, not even when it was first published. It was read as *argument*, a powerful argument, against the enslavement of three million African-Americans. In a broad, sentimental, two-dimensional way, by means of a simple, highly contrived story, fussy Victorian prose, and a cast of stereotyped white and black characters, the novel, in spite of its aesthetic and artistic limitations, somehow at least partially humanized for white Americans a people that had been utterly dehumanized, thus making the argument against slavery convincing for those hundreds of thousands of readers of popular fiction who up to that point had not thought much about the subject or whose opinions on the subject had depended upon the received opinions of their political leaders and clergy and other public spokesmen and spokeswomen.

The Jungle in many ways is as difficult to read today as *Uncle Tom's Cabin*. The workers are angelic, the bosses satanic, everyone wears either a white hat or a black hat, and as soon as the workers discover Socialism and organize themselves into labor unions, they all receive personality transplants and throw off their chains and triumphantly march from a Socialist rally shouting, "Chicago will be ours!" The prose is stilted and reads as if it's been badly translated from a novel by Maxim Gorky. For example, here is the opening scene, a Lithuanian workers' wedding party:

> Most fearful they are to contemplate, the expenses of this entertainment. They will certainly be over two hundred dollars, and may be three hundred; and three hundred dollars is more than the year's income of many a person in this room. There are able-bodied men here who work from early morning until late at night, in ice-cold cellars with a quarter of an inch of water on the floor—men who for six or seven months in the year never see the sunlight from Sunday afternoon till the next Sunday morning—and who cannot earn three hundred dollars in a year. There are little children here, scarce in their teens, who can hardly see the top of the work benches—whose

parents have lied to get them their places—and
who do not make the half of three hundred dollars a year, and perhaps not even the third of it.
And then to spend such a sum, all in a single day
of your life, at a wedding feast! (For obviously it is
the same thing, whether you spend it at once for
your own wedding, or in a long time, at the wed-
dings of all your friends.)

It is very imprudent, it is tragic—but, ah, it is
so beautiful!

Ah, indeed, it is all so beautiful. But in spite of
the importance of *Uncle Tom's Cabin* in the history of
race in America and the importance of *The Jungle* in
bringing about reforms in the early industrialization
of American food production, they are not novels I
myself would like to have written. There have been
many like them, and there will be many more, I'm
sure: novels that in the interests of justice, human
rights, and equality aspire to inspire significant political or social change and alter government policy.
They call for change at the center. We call them protest novels. And they are written with as close an eye
on the audience as the most calculating best seller
(for more honorable reasons, of course, than simply
to enrich the author).

A true novelist, that is to say, one who aspires to
create a work of narrative art, has no thought of his
or her audience. At least not when he or she is a novelist writing. Later, perhaps, when one has gone from

being a novelist writing to being an Author, that is, a person who has finished a novel and actually published it, one thinks of one's audience, naturally. Usually with anxiety, however, because it's too late by then to change anything. But not while actually engaged in the writing of the novel. Not when submitting oneself to the discipline and rigor and tradition of the history of the form, which require that one be at all times wholly honest and nonjudgmental and as intelligent as possible—that one be, as Henry James prescribed, a person "on whom nothing is lost."

Yet if the only kind of novel that seems capable of fostering change in the larger world is the protest novel—an argument disguised as a story, propaganda (for good or ill, it matters not) wrapped in narrative—why have so few serious literary artists deigned to write them? They can't be that difficult to write. Especially since the best of them, the most effective, appear to rely so heavily on stereotypes, clichés, sentiment, judgment, and slapdash prose. (Although, to be honest, unless one is making a parody, it's as difficult to write badly on purpose as it is to write well.)

Perhaps the reason so few serious literary artists try to write protest novels is that they feel it's simply not their job to foster change in the larger world, at least not by means of their literary works. Samuel Johnson in the eighteenth century declared in the preface to his dictionary that "the chief glory of every people arises from its authors." He did not mean ornamental glory, a cultural bauble whose existence points to a people's good taste and refinement. He meant that a people's expression of its essential nature depends upon its authors, its poets, storytellers, and novelists. For better or worse. Our authors' task is to describe us to ourselves and others. Without them we have no defined identity that distinguishes us from others and simultaneously ties us to them, all of them. To the living and the long dead and the yet unborn.

Thus the true task of the novelist is to dramatize first for himself or herself and ultimately for the rest of us what it is to be human in our time and for all time. What it is to be human in our place and in every place. As a species, we have always depended upon our storytellers to tell us what it means to be human. To be ourselves. The history of story, from the caves of Lascaux to the *Odyssey* and the *Iliad* to *The Sopranos* shows us this. And the history of one kind of story, especially, the novel, from Cervantes to Rushdie and DeLillo, makes this case even more explicitly than any other kind.

Our political leaders and moral arbiters, religious, corporate, and academic, would have us believe that human beings are fundamentally either right or wrong, good or evil, and that our behavior and beliefs, therefore, are meant to be prescribed, governed, arbitrated, and punished or rewarded by others, by those who, by virtue of their office, education, class status, or birthright, are more qualified to judge our behavior and beliefs than we ourselves are. The novel, especially, but all forms of story that are neither meant to be merely entertainment nor intended strictly to produce social or political change, deny this assumption.

Inasmuch as the novelist in the act of writing his or her novels opposes this view, the official view, he or she is a saboteur of received opinion. The serious novelist (who is often comic), by example and through his or her art, affirms the transcendent value of the individual and that individual's private consciousness of being briefly alive and not permanently dead. At the center of every morally ambitious novel is a vision of the supreme worth of one's secret, private consciousness, which, without the novel, is barely known, even to ourselves, much less acknowledged as significant to others. In this sense, and it is a crucially defining sense, today and in the past, and one hopes for as long as human beings tell stories to themselves and to one another, the novelist is at bottom committed to a life of opposition, of speaking truth to power, of challenging and overthrowing received wisdom and disregarding the official version of everything. This is why so many novelists have been censored, imprisoned, exiled, or even killed.

For the novelist does not speak in his books for others; the novelist *listens* to others. Especially to those who otherwise would go unheard. The novelist does not step forward in public to be seen by others; he *sees* others. Especially those who otherwise would remain invisible. And by his example, as well as by the work itself, he inspires others to listen and to see.

If by means of a novel the individual human being and his or her consciousness of being alive on this planet for a few flickering days or years or decades are signified—are made significant—then those who would deny that significance and all the rights and privileges that go with it will be seen as deaf and blind at best and as criminals at worst. A proper novel is both a celebration of the single, solitary human being and an indictment of those who refuse to join the celebration. The individual human being might be anyone—rich or poor, white or black, Christian or Muslim or Jew. He might be an atheist; a madman; a saint; or a common criminal. He might be monstrous or merely wicked; he might be a sap or a savant. He or she might be you. But when we enter the world of the novel in which he or she resides and live with him or her there for the duration, we will never see or hear his or her representative on earth again in the same way.

We know that things don't really change at the center; they merely get renovated. The bloody century just ended has taught us that much at least. It's as true even for protest novels like *The Jungle* and *Uncle Tom's Cabin* as for *Ulysses* and *The Sound and the Fury* and *One Hundred Years of Solitude*. Change occurs only at the edges, one human being at a time. And it occurs most significantly and in a viral, exponential way by means of words. Words made into sentences, sentences made into stories, stories made into novels.

I've spoken about the novelist as citizen, who is of course devoted to justice, human rights, and equality and, along with the rest of the intelligentsia, makes that easy vote. And the novelist as activist, as propagandist, if you will, whose writing is bent to a political purpose. And the novelist as artist, a person devoted strictly to the art of the novel. But what about the literary artist who is also what we call a "public intellectual"? Is that a possible role for a writer to play in our world today, or if a possible role, is it even necessary or useful—for the artist himself or herself, and for the larger community itself?

It's not at all unusual in Western Europe, South America, and Africa, and to some degree in Asian countries, too, for literary artists to find themselves invited to express in the media and to the people in charge of policy their considered opinions: on public affairs, on the issues of the day, on candidates running for political office, on foreign and domestic policy, and so forth. In most countries it's generally thought that literary artists are more likely than members of the governing class to possess the long view and that the long view is rather helpful in obtaining a more or less coherent short view. It's also generally thought that literary artists are less likely than policy makers to be beholden to what we call "special interests." Except, of course, when they themselves run for political office, like Mario Vargas Llosa, for instance, or Václav Havel, or the recently deceased Aimé Césaire of Martinique, or in the United States the previously mentioned Upton Sinclair, who ran for Congress as a Socialist and nearly became governor of California as an Independent. And then there was Norman Mailer's attempt to become the mayor of New York City. Interestingly, as soon as these figures ran for office, they lost all credibility as public intellectuals, and not until they were defeated, like Mailer and Vargas Llosa, or retired, like Havel, or died, did they regain it.

We in the United States have recently lost three of our public intellectuals (perhaps the final three, as there seems to be no one in the next younger generation to take their place)—Susan Sontag, Kurt Vonnegut, and Norman Mailer. They were literary artists of the first rank who spoke out early and often on matters of public policy, almost always taking unpopular positions, a few of which, I admit, might be regarded as downright weird (I'm speaking mostly of Mailer here), but overall, positions that in most cases were borne out by history as having been morally and socially correct, even if not always politically correct or economically expedient.

But the question is, Who in a position of power in the United States (except possibly J. Edgar Hoover when he was alive) cared what Sontag, Vonnegut, and Mailer had to say about AIDS, the Vietnam War, firebombing civilian populations, racism, the War on Terror, the invasion and occupation of Iraq, the torture of prisoners, the suspension of civil and constitutional rights, and on and on? If you don't count the writer's family and friends, practically no one cares. Yes, it's true that in a democratic republic like ours one can say and publish almost anything one wants to, but it's also true that, when the literary artist is regarded as a mere entertainer, only a little more essential to the commonweal than Michael Jackson and Britney Spears, a luxurious diversion, in other words, then he or she will end up marginalized, forced to speak solely to the choir. And when it comes to effecting change, effecting public policy, the choir, made up mostly of fellow artists and intellectuals, is essentially powerless.

By and large, our so-called public intellectuals nowadays operate out of think tanks and universities and hold to ideologically determined agendas, financed largely by the military-industrial complex of multinational corporations. They are sociologists and historians, scientists and bureaucrats, scholars and out-of-work journalists and policy wonks, paid to produce papers, articles, and books that will further the political ambitions of one or the other of our two political parties and the financial interests of corporate America. From time to time, one or another of them is invited to come up to the Big House and help run the plantation—think Paul Wolfowitz, Condoleezza Rice, Elliott Abrams. Mostly, they are lobbyists in sheep's clothing. They are certainly not poets, novelists, playwrights, or artists of any sort.

Our true poets, novelists, and dramatists, however, do not get to help run the plantation. Dr. Johnson's "chief glory of [the] people" is viewed by those in power as merely an ornamental glory, a cultural bauble that affirms our good taste and refinement, and for that the President now and then hangs gold medals around their necks at the Kennedy Center and says thanks for amusing us, now go on back to your sandbox and playthings so the adults can get on with the serious business of running the country and the world into the ground.

Not that I think our poets, novelists, and dramatists could run the country or the world much better than the present gang of miscreants and venal incompetents—although the idea of a Don DeLillo or John Ashbery or Tony Kushner as president has its attractions. I rather doubt we'd be mired in Iraq and Afghanistan or guarding the prisoners at Guantánamo if they were. Still, I wouldn't wish that fate on DeLillo, Ashbery, or Kushner—we need the moral and linguistic clarity of their writing more than we need their human decency in the White House. And that's the real problem, isn't it? We need decency in governance, and moral and linguistic clarity in literature.

Can the twain never meet? Honestly, I think not. Not anymore. Given the present and future dominance of democratic governments, and therefore of all public policy, by multinational corporate interests, it seems more than unlikely, it seems impossible, for the moral and linguistic clarity of our literary artists to have the slightest influence on the moral and linguistic imaginations of those who rule us.

The world, at least our world, seems to be breaking up into small colonies of the saved, as if we were entering a new Dark Age. If so, then perhaps the most important task we can set ourselves from here on out is to sustain, articulate, and preserve through literature the essential human values that early in the evolutionary history of our species distinguished us from our higher primate cousins—loving kindness, protection of the young, the weak, and the elderly, and consciousness of mortality. This is not something done by us in our capacity as citizens of one country or another or as voters one way or the other. Nor is it accomplished by protest novels, books like *The Jungle* and *Uncle Tom's Cabin*. And it has never been a particular concern of the writer in his or her role of public intellectual. Simply put, we must not be allowed to forget what it is to be human. The worst of it, what we share with our higher primate cousins, as well as the best of it, what we share with the angels.

No other species needs to be constantly reminded and taught what it is to be itself. And it is our storytellers, our poets, our novelists and dramatists, who have always performed this task. And surely, in this moment in the history of our species, when there is such a danger of forgetting and so much inducement to forget, we must not waste our limited time here doing anything else.

7

Talking to Strangers
Paul Auster

I don't know why I do what I do. If I did know, I probably wouldn't feel the need to do it. All I can say, and I say it with utmost certainty, is that I have felt this need since my earliest adolescence. I'm talking about writing, in particular writing as a vehicle to tell stories, imaginary stories that have never taken place in what we call the real world. Surely it is an odd way to spend your life—sitting alone in a room with a pen in your hand, hour after hour, day after day, year after year, struggling to put words on pieces of paper in order to give birth to what does not exist, except in your head. Why on earth would anyone want to do such a thing? The only answer I have ever been able to come up with is: because you have to, because you have no choice.

The need to make, to create, to invent is, no doubt, a fundamental human impulse. But to what end? What purpose does art, in particular the art of fiction, serve in what we call the real world? None that I can think of—at least not in any practical sense. A book has never put food in the stomach of a hungry child. A book has never stopped a bullet from entering a murder victim's body. A book has never prevented a bomb from falling on innocent civilians in the midst of war.

Some like to think that a keen appreciation of art can actually make us better people—more just, more moral, more sensitive, more understanding. Perhaps this is true—in certain rare, isolated cases. But let us not forget that Hitler started out in life as an artist. Tyrants and dictators read novels. Killers in prison read novels. And who is to say they don't derive the same enjoyment from books as everyone else?

In other words, art is useless, at least when compared, say, to the work of a plumber, or a doctor, or a railroad engineer. But is uselessness a bad thing? Does a lack of practical purpose mean that books and paintings and string quartets are simply a waste of our time? Many people think so. But I would argue that it is the very uselessness of art that gives it its value and that the making of art is what distinguishes us from all other creatures who inhabit this planet, that it is, essentially, what defines us as human beings.

To do something for the pure pleasure and beauty of doing it. Think of the effort involved, the long hours of practice and discipline required to become an accomplished pianist or dancer. All the suffering and hard work, all the sacrifices in order to achieve something that is utterly and magnificently . . . useless.

Fiction, however, exists in a somewhat different realm from the other arts. Its medium is language, and language is something we share with others, that is common to us all. From the moment we learn to talk, we begin to develop a hunger for stories. Those of us who can remember our childhoods will recall how ardently we relished the moment of the bedtime story, when our mother or father would sit down beside us in the semidark and read from a book of fairy tales.

Those of us who are parents will have no trouble conjuring with rapt attention in the eyes of our children when we read to them. Why this intense desire to listen? Fairy tales are often cruel and violent, featuring beheadings, cannibalism, grotesque transformations, and evil enchantments. One would think this material would be too frightening for a young child, but what these stories allow the child to experience is precisely an encounter with his own fears and inner torments in a perfectly safe and protected environment. Such is the magic of stories—they might drag us down to the depths of hell, but in the end they are harmless.

We grow older, but we do not change. We become more sophisticated, but at bottom we continue to resemble our young selves, eager to listen to the next story and the next, and the next. For years, in every country of the Western world, article after article has been published bemoaning the fact that fewer and fewer people are reading books, that we have entered what some have called the "postliterate age." That may well be true, but at the same time, this has not diminished the universal craving for stories.

Novels are not the only source, after all. Films and television and even comic books are churning out vast quantities of fictional narratives, and the public continues to swallow them up with great passion. That is because human beings need stories. They need them almost as desperately as they need food, and however the stories might be presented—whether on a printed page or a television screen—it would be impossible to imagine life without them.

Still, when it comes to the state of the novel, to the future of the novel, I feel rather optimistic. Numbers don't count where books are concerned. For there is only one reader, each and every time only one reader. That explains the particular power of the novel and why, in my opinion, it will never die as a form. Every novel is an equal collaboration between the writer and the reader, and it is the only place in the world where two strangers can meet on terms of absolute intimacy. I have spent my life in conversations with people I have never seen, with people I will never know, and I hope to continue until the day I stop breathing.

It's the only job I ever wanted.

8

Freedom to Write

Orhan Pamuk

Translated by Maureen Freely

In March 1985 Arthur Miller and Harold Pinter made a trip together to Istanbul. At the time, they were perhaps the two most important names in world theater, but unfortunately, it was not a play or a literary event that brought them to Istanbul but the ruthless limits being set on freedom of expression in Turkey at that time, and the many writers languishing in prison. In 1980 there was a coup in Turkey, and hundreds of thousands of people were thrown into prison, and as always, it was writers who were persecuted most vigorously. Whenever I've looked through the newspaper archives and the almanacs of that time to remind myself what it was like in those days, I soon come across the image that defines that era for most of us: men sitting in a courtroom, flanked by gendarmes, their heads shaven, frowning as their case proceeds. . . . There were many writers among them, and Miller and Pinter had come to Istanbul to meet with them and their families, to offer them assistance, and to bring their plight to the attention of the world. Their trip had been arranged by PEN in conjunction with the Helsinki Watch Committee. I went to the airport to meet them, because a friend of mine and I were to be their guides.

I had been proposed for this job not because I had anything to do with politics in those days but because I was a novelist who was fluent in English, and I'd happily accepted, not just because it was a way of helping writer friends in trouble but because it meant spending a few days in the company of two great writers. Together we visited small and struggling publishing houses, cluttered newsrooms, and the dark and dusty headquarters of small magazines that were on the verge of shutting down; we went from house to house, and restaurant to restaurant, to meet with writers in trouble and their families. Until then I had stood on the margins of the political world, never entering unless coerced, but now, as I listened to suffocating tales of repression, cruelty, and outright evil, I felt drawn to this world through guilt—drawn to it, too, by feelings of solidarity, but at the same time I felt an equal and opposite desire to protect myself from all this, and to do nothing in life but write beautiful novels. As we took Miller and Pinter by taxi from appointment to appointment through the Istanbul traffic, I remember how we discussed the street vendors, the horse carts, the cinema posters, and the scarfless and scarf-wearing women that are always so interesting to Western observers. But I clearly remember one image: at one end of a very long corridor in the Istanbul Hilton, my friend and I are whispering to each other with some agitation, while at the other end, Miller and Pinter are whispering in the shadows with the same dark intensity. This image remained engraved in my troubled mind, I think, because it illustrated the great distance between our complicated histories and theirs, while suggesting at the same time that a consoling solidarity among writers was possible.

I felt the same sense of mutual pride and shared shame in every other meeting we attended—room after room of troubled and chain-smoking men. I knew this because sometimes it was expressed openly, and sometimes I felt it myself or sensed it in other people's gestures and expressions. The writers, thinkers, and journalists with whom we were meeting mostly defined themselves as leftists in those days, so it could be said that their troubles had much to do with the freedoms held dear by Western liberal democracies. Twenty years on, when I see that half of these people—or thereabouts, I don't have the precise numbers—now align themselves with a nationalism that is at odds with Westernization and democracy, I of course feel sad.

My experience as a guide, and other like expe-

through them one by one, I could find none that I wished to explore "in my novels." But I knew, nonetheless, that if I said "There is nothing I wish to write in my novels that I am not able to discuss," I'd be giving the wrong impression. For I'd already begun to speak often and openly about all these dangerous subjects outside my novels. Moreover, didn't I often and angrily fantasize about raising these subjects in my novels, just because they happened to be forbidden? As I thought all this through, I was at once ashamed of my silence and reconfirmed in my belief that freedom of expression has its roots in pride and is, in essence, an expression of human dignity.

I have personally known writers who have chosen to raise forbidden topics purely because they were forbidden. I think I am no different. Because when another writer in another house is not free, no writer is free. This, indeed, is the spirit that informs the solidarity felt by PEN, by writers all over the world.

Sometimes my friends rightly tell me or someone else, "You shouldn't have put it quite like that; if only you had worded it like this, in a way that no one would find offensive, you wouldn't be in so much trouble now." But to change one's words and package them in a way that will be acceptable to everyone in a repressed culture, and to become skilled in this arena, is a bit like smuggling forbidden goods through customs, and as such, it is shaming and degrading.

The theme of this year's PEN festival is reason and belief. I have related all these stories to illustrate a

riences in later years, taught me something that we all know but that I would like to take this opportunity to emphasize. Whatever the country, freedom of thought and expression are universal human rights. These freedoms, which modern people long for as much as bread and water, should never be limited by using nationalist sentiment, moral sensitivities, or—worst of all—business or military interests. If many nations outside the West suffer poverty in shame, it is not because they have freedom of expression but because they don't. As for those who emigrate from these poor countries to the West or the North to escape economic hardship and brutal repression—as we know, they sometimes find themselves further brutalized by the racism they encounter in rich countries. Yes, we must also be alert to those who denigrate immigrants and minorities for their religion, their ethnic roots, or the oppression that the governments of the countries they've left behind have visited on their own people.

But to respect the humanity and religious beliefs of minorities is not to suggest that we should limit freedom of thought on their behalf. Respect for the rights of religious or ethnic minorities should never be an excuse to violate freedom of speech. We writers should never hesitate on this matter, no matter how "provocative" the pretext. Some of us have a better understanding of the West, some of us have more affection for those who live in the East, and some, like me, try to keep our hearts open to both sides of this slightly artificial divide, but our natural attachments and our desire to understand those unlike us should never stand in the way of our respect for human rights.

I always have difficulty expressing my political judgments in a clear, emphatic, and strong way—I feel pretentious, as if I'm saying things that are not quite true. This is because I know I cannot reduce my thoughts about life to the music of a single voice and a single point of view—I am, after all, a novelist, the kind of novelist who makes it his business to identify with all of his characters, especially the bad ones. Living as I do in a world where, in a very short time, someone who has been a victim of tyranny and oppression can suddenly become one of the oppressors, I know also that holding strong beliefs about the nature of things and people is itself a difficult enterprise. I do also believe that most of us entertain these contradictory thoughts simultaneously, in a spirit of goodwill and with the best of intentions. The pleasure of writing novels comes from exploring this peculiarly modern condition whereby people are forever contradicting their own minds. It is because our modern minds are so slippery that freedom of expression becomes so important: we need it to understand ourselves, our shady, contradictory, inner thoughts, and the pride and shame that I mentioned earlier.

So let me tell another story that might cast some light on the shame and pride I felt twenty years ago

while I was taking Miller and Pinter around Istanbul. In the ten years following their visit, a series of coincidences fed by good intentions, anger, guilt, and personal animosities led to my making a series of public statements on freedom of expression that bore no relation to my novels, and before long I had taken on a political persona far more powerful than I had ever intended. It was at about this time that the Indian author of a United Nations report on freedom of expression in my part of the world—an elderly gentleman—came to Istanbul and looked me up. As it happened, we, too, met at the Hilton Hotel. No sooner had we sat down at a table than the Indian gentleman asked me a question that still echoes strangely in my mind: "Mr. Pamuk, what is there going on in your country that you would like to explore in your novel but shy away from, due to legal prohibitions?"

There followed a long silence. Thrown by his question, I thought and thought and thought. I plunged into an anguished Dostoevskian self-interrogation. Clearly, what the gentleman from the UN wished to ask was, "Given your country's taboos, legal prohibitions, and oppressive policies, what is going unsaid?" But because he had—out of a desire to be polite, perhaps?—asked the eager young writer sitting across from him to consider the question in terms of his own novels, I, in my inexperience, took his question literally. In the Turkey of ten years ago, there were many more subjects kept closed by laws and oppressive state policies than there are today, but as I went

single truth—that the joy of freely saying whatever we want to say is inextricably linked with human dignity. So let us now ask ourselves how "reasonable" it is to denigrate cultures and religions or, more to the point, to mercilessly bomb countries, in the name of democracy and freedom of thought. My part of the world is not more democratic after all these killings. In the war against Iraq, the tyrannization and heartless murder of almost a hundred thousand people has brought neither peace nor democracy. To the contrary, it has served to ignite national-ist, anti-Western anger. Things have become a great deal more difficult for the small minority who are struggling for democracy and secularism in the Middle East. This savage, cruel war is the shame of America and the West. Organizations like PEN and writers like Harold Pinter and Arthur Miller are its pride.

9

Notes on Writing and the Nation
Salman Rushdie

1

The ousel singing in the woods of Cilgwri,
Tirelessly as a stream over the mossed stones,
Is not so old as the toad of Cors Fochno
Who feels the cold skin sagging round his bones.

Few writers are as profoundly engaged with their native land as R. S. Thomas, a Welsh nationalist, whose poems seek, by noticing, arguing, rhapsodizing, mythologizing, to write the nation into fierce, lyrical being. Yet this same R. S. Thomas also writes:

Hate takes a long time
To grow in, and mine

Has increased from birth;
Not for the brute earth. . .
I find
This hate's for my own kind.

Startling to find an admission of something close to self-hatred in the lines of a national bard. Yet this perhaps is the only kind of nationalist a writer can be. When the imagination is given sight by passion, it sees darkness as well as light. To feel so ferociously is to feel contempt as well as pride, hatred as well as love. These proud contempts, this hating love, often earn the writer a nation's wrath. The nation requires anthems, flags. The poet offers discord. Rags.

2

Connections have been made between the historical development of the twin "narratives" of the novel and the nation-state. The progress of a story through its pages toward its goal is likened to the self-image of the nation, moving through history toward its manifest destiny. Appealing as such a parallel is, I take it, these days, with a pinch of salt. Eleven years ago, at the famous PEN congress in New York City, the world's writers discussed "The Writer's Imagination and the Imagination of the State," a subject of Maileresque grandeur, dreamed up, of course, by Norman Mailer. Striking how many ways there were to read that little "and." For many of us, it meant "versus." South African writers—Gordimer, Coetzee—in those days of apartheid set themselves against the official definition of the nation. Rescuing, perhaps, the true nation from those who held it captive. Other writers were more in tune with their nations. John Updike sang an unforgettable hymn of praise to the little mailboxes of America, emblems, for him, of the free transmission of ideas. Danilo Kiš gave an example of a "joke" by the state: a letter received by him in Paris, posted in what was then still Yugoslavia. Inside the sealed envelope, stamped on the first page, were the words "This letter has not been censored."

3

The nation either co-opts its greatest writers (Shakespeare, Goethe, Camoëns, Tagore) or else seeks to destroy them (Ovid's exile, Soyinka's exile). Both fates are problematic. The hush of reverence is inappropriate for literature; great writing makes a great noise in the mind, the heart. There are those who believe that persecution is good for writers. This is false.

4

Beware the writer who sets himself or herself up as the voice of a nation. This includes nations of race, gender, sexual orientation, elective affinity. This is the New Behalfism. Beware behalfies!

The New Behalfism demands uplift, accentuates the positive, offers stirring moral instruction. It abhors the tragic sense of life. Seeing literature as inescapably political, it substitutes political values for literary ones. It is the murder of thought. Beware!

5

Be advised my passport's green.
America I'm putting my queer shoulder to the wheel.
To forge in the smithy of my soul the uncreated con-
    science of my race.

Kadare's Albania, Ivo Andrić's Bosnia, Achebe's Nigeria, García Márquez's Colombia, Jorge Amado's Brazil: writers are unable to deny the lure of the nation, its tides in our blood. Writing as mapping: the cartography of the imagination. (Or, as modern critical theory might spell it, Imagi/Nation.) In the best writing, however, a map of a nation will also turn out to be a map of the world.

6

History has become debatable. In the aftermath of Empire, in the age of superpower, under the "footprint" of the partisan simplifications beamed down to us from satellites, we can no longer agree on *what is the case,* let alone what it might mean. Literature steps into this ring. Historians, media moguls, politicians do not care for the intruder, but the intruder is a stubborn sort. In this ambiguous atmosphere, upon this trampled earth, in these muddy waters, there is work for him to do.

7

Nationalism corrupts writers, too. Vide Limonov's poisonous interventions in the war in former Yugoslavia. In a time of ever more narrowly defined nationalisms, of walled-in tribalisms, writers will be found uttering the war cries of their tribes. Closed systems have always appealed to writers. This is why so much writing deals with prisons, police forces, hospitals, schools. Is the nation a closed system? In this internationalized moment, can any system remain closed? Nationalism is that "revolt against history" which seeks to close what cannot any longer be closed. To fence in what should be frontierless.

Good writing assumes a frontierless nation. Writers who serve frontiers have become border guards.

8

If writing turns repeatedly toward nation, it just as repeatedly turns away. The deliberately uprooted intellectual (Naipaul) views the world as only a free intelligence can, going where the action is and offering reports. The intellectual uprooted against his will (a category that includes, these days, many of the finest Arab writers) rejects the narrow enclosures that have rejected him. There is a great loss, and much yearning, in such rootlessness. But there is also gain. The frontierless nation is not a fantasy.

9

Much great writing has no need of the public dimension. Its agony comes from within. The public sphere is as nothing to Elizabeth Bishop. Her prison—her freedom—her subject is elsewhere.

Lullaby.
Let nations rage,
Let nations fall.
The shadow of the crib makes an enormous cage
upon the wall.

10

The Sudden Sharp Memory
Ed Park

T: Do you feel well?

A: I'm not sure. I feel—dizzy.

T: An anxiety reaction, nothing more. Oh, the diz-
ziness is real, I grant you. But the cause is anxiety,
the sudden sharp memory.

A: May I rest? I'm tired now.

T: Are you retreating?

A: No. Really. But I'm dizzy and tired and my stomach feels queasy. I feel as though I've been here, in
this room, forever.

—*Robert Cormier,* I Am the Cheese *(1977). Banned by Leonard
Hall, Bay County, Florida, Schools Superintendent, 1985–1987*

A: Subject is a 38-year-old Asian male. He's wearing a hooded sweatshirt, jeans. He clutches a thin paperback, the edges of the pages blued, like they used to do. The title is *I Am the Cheese.*

(5-second interval)

All caps, letters the color of cheddar.

(8-second interval)

The cover shows a teenager on a bike. Knit cap, ragged military-style jacket. He looks like a cross between Edward Norton and Ryan from *The O.C.* On the front of his bike is a basket with something in it. The whole scene is washed out, nearly sepia. There's a man in the distance, looking at us, or him, but you can't make out the expression on his face. There's a thin line of shadow on the right of the tableau, like this is a photo or a print placed atop a white surface.

(5-second interval)

A ring of real iron keys interrupts the lower-right-hand corner. I mean, the keys lie on top of the picture just described. Already this book is playing with representation and reality.

E: You know I can hear every word you're saying, right? I'm sitting about two feet away.

A: I wondered when you were going to talk. You said nothing when I sat down.

E: I was reading.

(5-second interval)

Thinking.

(5-second interval)

I didn't know who to expect, what you would look like.

(3-second interval)

I've been waiting for this for a long time.

(10-second interval)

We're here. We're in this room. We might as well talk.

(5-second interval)

I assume this is being recorded?

A: You've brought a book. Why did you choose *I Am the Cheese*?

E: You make it sound like I had a choice. As soon as I knew that you wanted to talk about banned books, this was the one that came swimming out of the depths of my memory.

(5-second interval)

The other day I was thinking how memory itself is like a censor, as capricious and strict as any morality squad.

(5-second interval)

I'm just riffin'.

(3-second interval)

Why do I remember certain things, forget others? The ratio of remembered to forgotten must be like 1:5,000,000.

(5-second interval)

I didn't have a choice, really. It's all predestined. Like the nursery song the book takes its title from. The natural order. There's no escape.

(Sings softly)

"The farmer takes a wife, the farmer takes a wife . . ."

(3-second interval)

Then the wife takes the child, the child takes the cat, the cat takes the rat, the rat takes the cheese, and the cheese stands alone, which is also a lie. Because no, the cheese doesn't stand alone—it gets devoured. Annihilated.

(5-second interval)

Nice conflation of the food chain with family planning. And "takes" has all sorts of meanings. Proprietary. Sexual. Violent.

(5-second interval)

Great fucking title.

(6-second interval)

A: Why don't you tell me about the book? Then we'll talk about—

(12-second interval)

Are you feeling OK?

(5-second interval)

Do you wish to suspend?

(5-second interval)

Let us suspend then.

END TAPE AE001

TAPE AE001 1130   **date deleted** _____

A: Is this the copy that you read as a kid?

E: Yes. Look at the edges—that turquoise color. It's lighter along the top, from where the sun hit it. Now look at this gorgeous color here, the long edge. Beautiful. Makes me nostalgic.

A: For what?

E: I don't know. The age of turquoise page edges. Somewhere there's a grad student doing her dissertation on the inks used in twentieth-century mass-market paperbacks.
(6-second interval)
This edition is copyright 1981. The novel was first published in 1977. I'd say I read it in '82 or '83, when I was twelve, maybe thirteen. I forget exactly. No later than fourteen. I didn't keep a journal then. I should have written all this stuff down.
(3-second interval)
It's crazy how much you forget.
(8-second interval)
These blurbs are great. "A bike-ride through a Twilight Zone." *Kirkus.* "Simply one of the best novels, dot dot dot, this year." *Newsweek.*
(6-second interval)
Dot dot dot.
(6-second interval)
That's what *I Am the Cheese* is all about, really. *Dot dot dot.* Gaps. Lacunae. It's a kid trying to fill in the

blanks of his life. Do you know the story? Can I tell you the story? I won't tell you what happens at the very end.

A: I don't mind spoilers.

E: Trust me, you don't want me to tell you. You need
to read it yourself.
    (3-second interval)
I was rereading the book last month, and I remembered it had a doozy of an ending, a huge twist, but I'd forgotten exactly what it was. I should have figured it out, of course, this time around, but I didn't. Then I got to the end and it *blindsided* me.
    (6-second interval)
Some people don't like twists. I love twists.
    (3-second interval)
So I'm not going to tell you about the end but I'll tell you the highlights. And then I guess we should talk about what it means that this book got banned.
    (4-second interval)
So in *I Am the Cheese,* the protagonist, who is also the narrator of parts of the book—actually, I'll get to that in a sec—is a kid named Adam Farmer. He lives in Monument, Massachusetts, with his insurance-agent father and vaguely sad mother. He's bookish, shy, enjoys old things, wants to be a writer someday like Thomas Wolfe—not the "hip writer" Tom Wolfe.
    (3-second interval)

I had no idea what that meant when I read it. I mean, I didn't know who Tom Wolfe was. And when I eventually encountered his writing, I couldn't get that "hip writer" tag out of my mind!

(3-second interval)

Anyway, Adam meets a girl named Amy Hertz. An extrovert. Mischievous. Somehow she takes a shine to him. One day her father has a visitor from another town—the small town where Adam was born. She asks the visitor if he'd ever heard of Adam's folks, and he says he hasn't. Which is strange, for someone who's lived in such a small town all his life.

(6-second interval)

Things unravel from there. In a nutshell, Adam's real last name isn't Farmer. His father used to be a newspaper reporter, who uncovered links between organized crime and the state government. The mob forced him to enter the witness protection program, change his name and profession, move his family. He had to cut off all ties to his past life.

(3-second interval)

It's probably inevitable that Adam would learn all this, but the way Cormier structures the book, his eureka breaks over him slowly, coming as a series of smaller discoveries—of incongruities, deceptions. And of course *he's* deceiving his parents, sneaking around to puzzle together his real life.

(15-second interval)

Isn't that what all kids do, when they hit adolescence? Try to tease out the truth about their parents, about themselves? Cormier took this impulse and turned it paranoid.

(6-second interval)

It's one of the most paranoid books I've ever read.

(3-second interval)

It *should* be banned! *(Laughs.)*

(3-second interval)

Wait. Look at this blurb, from *Booklist*: "Cormier's theme of one person against overwhelming organizational odds is developed here with stunning force." That word: "organizational." I want to riff on that. Can I riff? Do I have permission for riffage?

(3-second interval)

OK. So think about the organization of a book. Most books we read are pretty straightforward in this regard. A voice, a tone, is established, a simple time frame adhered to, and if the author's any good she can push this narrative strategy through to the end, keeping the reader under her spell.

(4-second interval)

The radical thing about *I Am the Cheese*, for a twelve-year-old reader, is that though the language can be intense—not in terms of curse words but in terms of emotional drama—Cormier's actually getting much of his effect from his *organization* of the material. For "organizational odds," read "odd organization." He kicks off the book with a present-tense, first-person voice—Adam's—recounting our hero's quest to find his father. He's biking from Monument to Rutterburg, Vermont, with a package, a gift, for his father. He's running away—but from where?

(3-second interval)

After a couple of pages, Cormier breaks the spell. Now we are reading the transcript of an interview between Adam and someone—a doctor perhaps, a psychiatrist—named Brint. Gaps of assorted duration—"5-second interval," "12-second interval"—punctuate the exchange, and it's in these silences that the mystery *breathes*. It's breathtakingly creepy and effective.

(5-second interval)

What does Brint want? Why does Adam keep having headaches, withholding information?

(3-second interval)

There's yet a *third* element to the organization of *I Am the Cheese,* and that's the swaths of third-person, past-tense narrative that often interrupt the transcripts, as if a flashback is playing in Adam's head while he zones out in front of the interviewer. Cormier swings freely between these three narrative conceits, and what's cool is how the story falls into place in three different time frames, which then overlap, snap into focus. But it's not just "what happens" that works so well. It's the *gaps,* see. You experience the story the way Adam learns about his life—confronting these blanks, the disjunctures between narratives, that your mind works to fill in.

(6-second interval)

Not only that, but the very strategy of toggling

among three different narratives—three different states of mind—keeps you on your toes, the way Adam becomes alert to every change in his daily life. The rug keeps getting pulled out from under you. You can't settle into one groove, one way of thinking.

(5-second interval)

I'm getting really excited talking about this.

(6-second interval)

I'd like to stop for today.

A: Would you like some water? We can break for a few minutes.

(5-second interval)

I'd really like to keep going.

(15-second interval)

This is great stuff.

(8-second interval)

I'd really like for you to continue, Ed.

(5-second interval)

Let us suspend.

END TAPE AE002

TAPE AE003 1130   **date deleted _____**

A: This was a banned book when you were growing up?

E: The whole *Cheese* controversy happened a few years later, down in Florida. In 1985 a grandmother in Bay County sent a letter to the school superintendent. Something Hall—Leonard Hall. She said she found the book immoral—for bad language, and because it advanced "humanism and behaviorism."

(5-second interval)

Isn't "humanism" a good thing?

(4-second interval)

I'm not even sure what she means by "behaviorism."

(3-second interval)

Hall had the book banned, even though nearly all the students had received parental permission to read it for their English class. It was something of a progressive school, from what I understand.

(3-second interval)

This is all in a book called *What Johnny Shouldn't Read*. Chapter seven.

(3-second interval)

I have it right here, actually.

(3-second interval)

Another adult, I guess the actual parent of the girl with the offended grandmother, filled out a form— a "Request for Reconsideration of Instructional Materials"—calling *I Am the Cheese* "morbid and depressing," and objecting to its "crude and vulgar" language. The father of this adult—Collins—also joined the fray. This is what's in the book:

[Collins's] letter, dated May 22, 1986, charged that novels used in the program contain "obscene language and sexual explicities [*sic*]." He amplified his views in a newspaper interview: '"There's no respect in this county any more,' Collins said. 'You cannot go down the halls of the high schools and junior highs without hearing the dirtiest language you ever heard in your life. I believe these filthy little books are the cause.'"

(10-second interval)

A committee consisting of teachers and the parents of Mowat students voted to reinstate the book, but Hall rejected this. It stayed banned, things snowballed.

(3-second interval)

I kind of don't want to go through the whole thing now. It's too depressing.

(3-second interval)

But basically it's a minority of adults trying to place restrictions on student reading, based on whether the books fit into their particular form of morality.

(3-second interval)

I mean it's stupid, right? Of course it is. But it's interesting how the book they chose to ban, *I Am the Cheese,* is *about* forbidden knowledge. What gets covered up, distorted. What we pretend does not exist. Today I read that absence into those gaps between the different narrative sections, and into those silences that blossom in the interview transcripts. It's like the censors had unconsciously found the perfect mirror to their censorship.

(17-second interval)

I like what Nietzsche said about the writings of antiquity: They're the only ones that modern man reads *with exactness*.

(6-second interval)

The same could be said of banned books.

(3-second interval)

Also I was thinking that maybe the gaps in the interview tapes are residue from Watergate? And the plot as a whole, too—about how you can't trust the government. Remember, this is the mid-seventies so all that stuff is fresh in Cormier's mind.

(3-second interval)

I'm just riffin'.

(3-second interval)

Maybe we'll talk about it later.

END TAPE AE003

11

Witness: The Inward Testimony
Nadine Gordimer

September 2001. A sunny day in New York. Many of us who are writers were at work on the transformations of life into a poem, story, a chapter of a novel, when terror pounced from the sky, and the world made witness to it.

"*HORROR was written on the sun*"[1]

The prophetic words of the poet William Plomer.

The horrors of Hiroshima and Nagasaki were part of the unspeakable horrors of a past war; *this* was the horror that had come with the arrival of a new kind of war in a new millennium that has dedicated itself to globalization—a concept which both implies and is absolutely reliant on an end to violent solutions of international conflict. It is now 2008: we have come to coexist with the horrors of Madrid bombings,

London underground train explosions, the dead in Afghanistan, Rwanda, Darfur, Sri Lanka . . . the list does not close.

What place, task, meaning will literature have in witness to disasters without precedence in the manner in which these destroy deliberately and pitilessly, with the entire world the front line of any and every conflict?

Place. Task. Meaning.

To apportion these for us, the world's writers, I believe we have first to define what *witness* is.

No simple term.

I go to the *Oxford English Dictionary* and find that definitions fill more than five small-print columns. "*Witness*": "attestation of a fact, event, or statement; testimony, evidence; . . . one who is or was present and is able to testify from personal observation."

Television crews, photographers, are preeminent witnesses in these senses of the word, when it comes to catastrophe, staggeringly visual. No need for words to describe it; no possibility words *could*.

Firsthand newsprint, elaborately descriptive journalism becomes essentially a pallid afterimage. Television makes "personal observation, attestation of a fact, event" a qualification of witness not only for those thousands who stood mind-blown aghast on the scene but for everyone worldwide who saw it all happening on television.

The place and task of attesting the fact, event, or statement, testimony, evidence—the qualification of one who is or was present and is able to testify—this is that of the media. Analysis of the disaster follows in political, sociological terms, by various ideological, national, special, or populist schemas, some claiming that elusive reductive state, objectivity. And to the contexts—political, sociological—in this case, according to the dictionary there must be added analysis in religious terms. For number 8 in the list of definitions cites: "One who testifies for Christ or the Christian faith, esp. by death, a martyr." The *Oxford English Dictionary,* conditioned by Western Christian culture, naturally makes the curious semantic decision to confine this definition of the term *witness* to one faith only. But the perpetrators of terrorist attacks often testify as witness, in this sense, to another faith—a faith which the dictionary does not recognize: to the faith of Islam, by death and martyrdom.

Place, task; meaning.

Meaning is what cannot be reached by the immediacy of the image, the description of the sequence of events, the methodologies of expert analysis. If witness literature is to find its place, take on a task in relation to the enormity of what is happening in acts of mass destruction and their aftermath, it is in the tensions of sensibility, the intense awareness, the antennae of receptivity to the lives among which writers experience their own as a source of their art. Poetry and fiction are processes of what the *Oxford Dictionary* defines the state of witness as "applied to the inward testimony"—the individual lives of men, women, and children who have to reconcile within themselves the shattered certainties which are as much a casualty as the bodies under rubble in New York and the dead in Afghanistan.

Kafka says the writer sees among ruins "different (and more) things than others . . . it is a leap out of murderers' row; it is a seeing of what is really taking place."[2]

This is the nature of witness that writers can, surely must, give, have been giving since ancient times, in the awesome responsibility of their endowment with the seventh sense of the imagination. The "realization" of what has happened comes from what would seem to deny reality—the transformation of events, motives, emotions, reactions, from the immediacy into the enduring significance that is meaning.

If we accept that "contemporary" spans the century in which all of us here were born, as well as the one scarcely and starkly begun, there are many examples of this fourth dimension of experience that is the writer's space and place attained.

"Thou shalt not kill": the moral dilemma that patriotism and religions demand be suppressed in the individual sent to war, comes inescapably from the First World War pilot in W. B. Yeats's poem:

> Those that I fight I do not hate,
> Those that I guard I do not love.[3]

A leap from murderers' row that only the poet can make.

The Radetzky March and *The Emperor's Tomb*—
Joseph Roth's peripatetic duel epic of the frontiers
as the Charybdis and Scylla of the breakup of the
old world in disintegration of the Austro-Hungarian
Empire, is not only inward testimony of the ever-
lengthening host of ever-wandering refugees into the
new century, the Greek chorus of the dispossessed
that drowns the muzak of consumerism. It is the
inward testimony of what goes on working its way as
a chaos of ideological, ethnic, religious and political
consequences—Bosnia, Kosovo, Macedonia—that
come to us through the vision of Roth.

The statistics of the Holocaust are a ledger of evil,
the figures still visible on people's arms; but Primo
Levi's *If This Is a Man* makes extant *a state of existence* that becomes part of consciousness for all time.
Part unavoidably of the tangled tragic justifications
made behind the violence perpetrated in the Israeli-
Palestinian conflict.

The primal cause of human inhumanity to humans,
which was about to epitomize in the fall of atom
bombs in Japan, is foreshadowed and encompassed in
Kenzaburo Oe's World War II story where a black
American survives the crash of an American fighter
plane in a remote district of Japan and is discovered by
villagers. None has ever seen a black man before.

"He's black, you see that. . . . he's a real black man . . ."

"What are they going to do with him, shoot him?"

"Because he's the enemy," asserts the narrator, a
child of the village.

But his father says, "Until we know what the town thinks, rear him."

"Rear him? Like an animal?"

"He's the same as an animal," the father says gravely. "He stinks like an ox."

The man is chained to a wild boar trap and kept in a cellar; the small boys are delegated to take him food and empty his sanitary pail. Totally dehumanized: "The black soldier began to exist in the cellar for the sole purpose of filling the children's daily lives." They are fascinated by and terrified of him, until one day they find him tinkering with the boar trap with the manual skill they recognize from the abilities of their own people. "He's like a person," one boy says. They secretly bring him a toolbox. He works to free his legs. "We sat next to him and he looked at us, then his large yellow teeth were bared and his cheeks slackened and we were jolted by the discovery that he could also smile. We understood then that we had been joined to him by a sudden deep, passionate bond that was almost 'human.'"[4] Oe's genius of inward testimony goes even deeper in not turning away from the aleatory circumstances—otherness, its definitive in war—which end in the captive using the boy brutally as a human shield when the adults come to kill him.

And the monitored and measured accounts of distortion, mutation of living organisms, human, animal, and plant life, down generations, which was to come as the result of atomic explosion, find the shudder of *meaning* in a single flower: another Japanese writer, Masuji Ibuse, writes of an iris appearing out of season. "From . . . the angular leaves emerged the twisted stem with its belated, purple flower. The petals looked hard and crinkly. No wonder I had mistaken them for tissue paper."[5] And a friend says, "The iris in this pond is crazy and belongs to a crazy age!"

The level of unflinching imaginative tenacity at which the South African poet Mongane Wally Serote witnessed the apocalyptic events of the apartheid amid which he was living is also organic, in its persistent perception. He writes,

> *I want to look at what happened;*
> *That done,*
> *As silent as the roots of plants pierce the soil*
> *I look at what happened. . .*
> *When knives creep in and out of people*
> *As day and night into time.*[6]

In an earlier age, Conrad's inward testimony finds that the heart of darkness is not Mistah Kurtz's skull-bedecked river station besieged by Congolese but back in the offices in King Leopold's Belgium where knitting women sit while the savage trade in natural rubber is efficiently organized, with a quota for extraction by blacks that must be met, or punished at the price of severed hands.

These are some examples of what Czeslaw Milosz

calls the writer's "fusing of individual and historical elements"[7] and what Georg Lukács defines as the occurrence of "a creative memory which transfixes the object and transforms it," "the duality of inwardness and the outside world."[8]

I have spoken of the existential condition of the writer of witness literature in the way in which I would define that literature. The question raises a hand: How much has the writer been involved in his or her own flesh-and-blood person, at risk in the radical events, social upheavals, the threats to the very bases of life and dignity? How much must the writer be involved? In a terrorist attack, anyone present in the air or on earth is at risk, be come activist-as-victim. No choice of being any kind of observer. In other terrible events—the wars, social upheavals, for good or bad ends—like anyone else the writer may be a victim, no choice. But the writer, like anyone else, may have chosen to be a protagonist. As witness in her or his own person, victim or protagonist, is that writer not unquestionably the one from whom the definitive witness literature must come?

Albert Camus believed so.

Camus believed that his comrades in the French Resistance who had experienced so much that was physically, mentally, both spiritually devastating and strengthening, appallingly revealing, would produce writers who would bring all this to literature and into the consciousness of the French as no other form of witness could. He waited in vain for the writer to emerge. The extremity of human experience does not make a writer. An Oe surviving atomic blast and fall-out, a Dostoevsky reprieved at the last moment before a firing squad; the predilection has to be there, as a singer is endowed with a certain kind of vocal cords, a boxer is endowed with aggression. Primo Levi could be speaking of these fellow writers as well as himself, as an inmate of Auschwitz, when he realizes that theirs are stories each to be told "of a time and condition that cannot be understood except in the manner in which . . . we understand events of legends . . ."[9]

THE DUALITY OF INWARDNESS and the outside world: that is the one essential existential condition of the writer as witness. Marcel Proust certainly would be regarded by most as the one among real writers least confronted by any kind of public event; critics seem to ignore that the cork-lined room to which they confine him did not exclude the invasion of the Faubourg Saint-Germain of his novel by the most tellingly brilliant revelations of anti-Semitism among the most privileged and powerful in France. So I am not daunted by any raised eyebrows when I accept, from Proust, a signpost for writers in our context: "The march of thought in the solitary travail of artistic creation proceeds downwards, into the depths, in the only direction that is not closed to us, along which we are free to advance—towards the goal of truth."[10]

Writers cannot and do not indulge the hubris of believing they can plant the flag of truth on that ineluctable territory. But what is sure is that we can exclude or discard nothing in our solitary travail towards meaning, downward into the acts of terrorism. We have to seek this meaning in those who commit such acts just as we do in its victims. We have to acknowledge them. Graham Greene's priest in *The Comedians* gives a religious edict from his interpretation of the Christian faith: "The Church condemns violence, but it condemns indifference more harshly." And another of his characters, Dr. Magiot, avows, "I would rather have blood on my hands than water like Pilate."[11]

There are many, bearing witness in one dictionary definition and another, who remind the world that the United States of America, victim of ghastly violence, has had on its hands the water of indifference to the cosmic gap between its prosperity and the conditions of other populations—a recent survey showed the richest 10 percent of 25 million (plus) Americans had a combined income greater than the combined income of 43 percent of the poorest of the world's population.[12]

Georg Büchner's character in the play *Danton's Death* makes a chilling declaration: "Terror is an outgrowth of virtue . . . the revolutionary government is the despotism of freedom against the tyranny of kings."[13]

Where does the despotism of terrorism begin to

grow; why? And where will it end? How? This is the mined territory of meaning, in the crisis of the present, from which the writer's responsibility cannot be absolved. "Servitude, falsehood and terror. . . . Three afflictions are the cause of silence between men, obscure them from one another and prevent them from rediscovering themselves."[14] That is what Camus found in that territory. It is a specification within Milan Kundera's credo: "For a novelist, a given historical situation is an anthropological laboratory in which he explores the basic question: What is existence?" And Kundera goes on to quote Heidegger: "The essence of man has the form of a question."[15]

Whether this question is unanswerable, just as final truth is unattainable, literature has been and remains a means of people rediscovering themselves. Which may be part of the answer to terrorism and the violent response it evokes. It has never been more necessary, vital, than now, when information technology, the new faith, has failed to bring this rediscovery about.

IS THERE INEVITABLY A loss of artistic liberty for the writer in inward testimony as witness?

A testy outburst not from a writer but a painter, Picasso, replies, vis-à-vis their creativity, for artists in every medium. "What do you think an artist is? An imbecile who has nothing but eyes if he is a painter or ears if he is a musician, or a lyre at every level of his heart if he is a poet . . . quite the contrary, he is at the same time a political being, constantly aware of what goes on in the world, whether it be harrowing, bitter or sweet, and he cannot help being shaped by it."[16] Neither can the art. And there emerges *Guernica.*

Flaubert writes to Turgenev: "I have always tried to live in an ivory tower, but a tide of shit is beating at its walls, threatening to undermine it."[17]

Witness literature is not anathema to, incompatible with experiment in form and style, the marvelous adventures of the word. On the contrary, when writers, as André Pieyre de Mandiargues asks, "have been given a disaster which seems to exceed all measures, must it not be recited, spoken?" in response the writer has to wrestle with all the possibilities of his medium, the Word, to find the one way in which the demands of *meaning* can be recited, spoken.[18]

There is no style and form ready-made for witness literature. If it is to be a poem, it has to be found among all the combinations of poetics, tried or never tried, to be equal to the unique expression that will contain the event *before and beyond the event;* its past and future. As Yeats did with his pilot at war. If witness is to be a story or novel, that final demand—the expression of the event before and beyond the event—is the same. Among all the ways of plumbing meaning, existing and to be, this has to be discovered. Julio Corázar, Carlos Fuentes, Gabriel García Márquez, Kenzaburo Oe, Octavio Paz, José Saramago—these are writers who discovered it unsurpassably for their own people, own countries, and, by the boundlessness of great writing, for the rest of us who see the same responsibility of discovery to be pursued in our own countries.

I have had my own experience as that of being a writer given evidence of a disaster which seemed to exceed all measure. In South Africa racism in its brutally destructive guises, from killing in conquest to the methodology of colonialism, certified as Divine Will by religious doctrine, took the lives of thousands of Africans and stunted the lives of millions more, *systematically*. I grew up in the Union that came out of wars for possession between the British and descendants of the Dutch, the Boers. The Africans had already been dispossessed by both. I was the child of the white minority, blinkered in privilege and conditioning education, basic as ABC. But because I was a writer—for it's an early state of being, before a word has been written, not an attribute of being published—I became witness to the *unspoken* in my society. Very young I entered a dialogue with myself about what was around me; and this took the form of trying for the meaning in what I saw by transforming this into stories based on what were everyday incidents of ordinary life for everyone around me: the sacking of the backyard room of a black servant by police while the white master and mistress of the house looked on unconcerned; later, in my adolescence during the '39–'45 War, when I was a voluntary aide at a gold mine casualty station, being told by the white intern who was suturing a black miner's gaping head wound without anesthetic, "They don't feel pain like we do."

As time and published books confirmed that I was a writer, and witness of literature, if it is a particular genre of my circumstance of my time and place, was mine, I had to find how to keep my integrity to the Word, the sacred charge of the writer. I realized, as I believe many writers do, that instead of restricting, inhibiting, coarsely despoiling aesthetic liberty, the existential condition of witness was enlarging, inspiring aesthetic liberty, breaching the previous limitations of my sense of form and use of language through necessity: to create form and sense anew.

In the Fifties, a story written almost anecdotally tried for inward testimony of the delivery from the mortuary of a body—any black man's body would do, instead of that of the father of a laborer on a white man's farm; here was the denial of possession of even six feet of the country, a grave-size share, to its rightful owner. In the 1970s, when the dispossession of Africans of their country reached its final entrenchment under apartheid, I found myself writing a novel for which only some combined form of lyricism and its antithesis, irony, could try for the meaning of land, buried this time with the body of an unknown black man on a white man's rural retreat, and rising, in the river's flood, a corpse to claim it. The apparently obsessive return to the theme—literally the ground of colonialism on which I lived—was both subconscious

in the writer's lifetime love affair with the possibilities of the Word *and* an imperative from the condition of witness.

Aesthetic liberty is an essential of witness literature if it is to fulfill its justification as *meaning*. And
the form and use of language that will be the expression for one piece of work will not serve for another.
When next I wrote a novel, it was, in terms of witness literature, an exploration of inward testimony to
revolutionary political dedication as a faith like any
religious faith, with edicts not to be questioned by any
believer, and the consequences of this, the existential
implications handed down from father to daughter,
mother to son. Witness called on aesthetic liberty to
find the form and language, in order for the narrative
to be fulfilled in meaning. Lyricism and irony would
not serve where a daughter's inner survival of personality depended on fully recovering her father's life
of willing martyrdom, his loving relationship with
her and its calculating contradictions in the demands
his highest relationship, political faith, made upon
her; his actions, motives, other personal attachments,
which the condition of revolutionary clandestin-
ity perforce made a mystery. A work where, indeed,
actual documents must be encompassed to be deci-
phered in terms of inward testimony. Through aesthetic liberty I had, so to speak, to question this story
in many inner voices, to tell it in whatever I might
reach of its own meaning, submerged beneath public

ideology, discourse, and action. Not a psychological but an aesthetic quest.

There is no ivory tower that can keep the assault of reality from beating at the walls, as Flaubert dismayedly noted. In witness to it the imagination is not irreal but is the deeper reality. Its exigence can never allow compromise with conventional cultural wisdom and what Milosz calls official lies. That outstanding intellectual of no compromise Edward Said asks who, if not the writer, is "to uncover and elucidate the contests, challenge and hope to defeat the imposed silence and normalized quiet of power?"[19] And the final word on witness literature surely comes from Camus: "The moment when I am no more than a writer I shall cease to be a writer."[20]

1. William Plomer, "Manifesto," *Turbott Wolfe*

2. Franz Kafka, *Diaries 1921*

3. W. B. Yeats, "An Irish Airman Foresees His Death," in *Collected Poems*

4. Kenzaburo Oe, "Prize Stock," in *Teach Us to Outgrow Our Madness*

5. Masuji Ibuse, "The Crazy Iris," *The Crazy Iris & Other Stories of Atomic Aftermath*. Edited by Kenzaburo Oe

6. Mongane Wally Serote, "Ofay-Watcher Looks Back," *Yakhal 'inkomo*

7. Czeslaw Milosz, *Native Realm*

8. Georg Lukács, *Theory of The Novel*

9. Primo Levi

10. Marcel Proust, "Within a Budding Grove," *In Search of Time Lost*
11. Graham Greene, *The Comedians*
12. *Human Development Report 2001,* United Nations Development Programme
13. Georg Büchner, *Danton's Death*
14. Albert Camus, *The Rebel*
15. Milan Kundera, Postcript to *Life Is Elsewhere*
16. Pablo Picasso, *Letters Françaises*
17. Gustave Flaubert, Letter to Turgenev, *The Letters of Flaubert, 1857–80,* edited by Francis Steegmuller
18. André Pieyre de Mandiargues, *The Margin*
19. Edward Said
20. Albert Camus, *Notebooks*

CONTRIBUTORS

Paul Auster was born in Newark, New Jersey, on February 3, 1947. He is the author of numerous novels, screenplays, and works of nonfiction. His latest novel, *Man in the Dark*, was published in 2008. He lives in Brooklyn, New York, with his wife, the author Siri Hustvedt. His piece in this collection, "Talking to Strangers," was delivered as an acceptance speech for the Prince of Asturias Prize for literature in October 2006.

Russell Banks is the founding president of Cities of Refuge North America and a member of the American Academy of Arts and Letters and the American Academy of Arts and Sciences. His work has been translated into twenty languages and has received numerous international prizes and awards. He lives in upstate New York and is the New York State Author.

Nadine Gordimer, born November 20, 1923, is a South African writer and has been a strong voice in politics and in the literary world since the 1960s. She published her first story at the age of fifteen, and was active in the antiapartheid movement as well as a member of the African National Congress. She is vice president of International PEN, and in 1991 she was awarded the Nobel Prize in Literature. Her novels include *The Pickup, July's People,* and *The Conservationist.*

David Grossman is an Israeli author of fiction, non-fiction, and children's literature. He has been an advocate for peace in Israel. He has been honored with the Geschwister Scholl Prize as well as the degree doctor honoris causa. He is the author of the much acclaimed *See Under: Love, The Book of Intimate Grammar,* and *The Yellow Wind,* as well as *Someone to Run With.*

Pico Iyer has been chronicling the global order for twenty-five years, in books such as *Video Night in Kathmandu, The Global Soul,* and, most recently, *The Open Road,* describing thirty-three years of talks and travels with the Fourteenth Dalai Lama.

Orhan Pamuk was born in Istanbul in 1952. At the age of twenty-three he decided to become a novelist, and giving up everything else retreated into his flat and began to write. His books have been translated into more than fifty languages. He is the winner of the Nobel Prize in Literature for 2006, the second youngest person to receive the award in its history. Pamuk's novel *My Name Is Red* won the 2003 IMPAC Dublin Literary Award. He lives in Istanbul.

Ed Park is the author of a novel, *Personal Days*, and a founding editor of *The Believer*. He lives in New York.

Francine Prose is the author of the *New York Times* best seller *Reading Like a Writer* as well as fourteen books of fiction, including *A Changed Man,* winner of the Dayton Literary Peace Prize, and *Blue Angel,* a finalist for the National Book Award. Her latest book is *Goldengrove.* A distinguished critic and essayist, she has taught literature and writing for more than twenty years at major universities. She is currently president of the PEN American Center board of trustees and lives in New York City.

Salman Rushdie, one of the best known anticensorship literary figures of our time, served as president of the PEN American Center from 2004 to 2006 and continues to work as president of the PEN World Voices International Literary Festival, which he helped create. His many literary prizes include the Best of the Booker, Whitbread Prize for Best Novel (twice), and the Aristeion Prize. He holds the rank of Commandeur in the Ordre des Arts et des Lettres, France's highest artistic honor. In June 2007 he was knighted for services to literature. Rushdie's works include *Midnight's Children, The Satanic Verses, Shalimar* *the Clown*, and *The Enchantress of Florence*. His books have been translated into more than forty languages.

John Updike, the novelist, poet, and critic, was considered one of America's "premier men of letters." He won two Pulitzer Prizes and was one of the few Americans to be honored with both the National Medal of Art and the National Medal for the Humanities. He published more than sixty books, including *Rabbit, Run; Rabbit Is Rich;* and *Rabbit at Rest.*

About PEN

PEN is the leading voice for literature and a major force for free expression and the unhampered exchange of ideas and opinions worldwide. Founded in 1921, it is the world's oldest ongoing human rights organization, and it currently has 144 PEN centers in 102 countries dedicated to protecting the right of all humanity to create and communicate freely. By mobilizing the world's most influential literary voices and an international network of writers, readers, and human rights supporters, PEN makes a difference every day in the lives of writers who are facing persecution around the world. For more information about PEN, visit www .pen.org.

ABOUT THE EDITOR

Toni Morrison was awarded the Nobel Prize for Literature in 1993. She is the author of many novels, including *Sula, Song of Solomon, Beloved,* and, most recently, *A Mercy.* She has also received the National Book Critics Circle Award and a Pulitzer Prize for her fiction.